CHAPTER1

The Second World War was in full swing when my mother gave birth to twin boys in a nursing home in Frindsbury, in the county of Kent, England. My name is Douglas, and I was one of those twins. The other was named Peter. He died when we were both only a few months old.

My mother brought six children into the world and, sadly, lost two of them to illness during their early years. Peter was one. Another brother, Brian, also passed away in childhood.

The birth itself was a difficult one. Twins were not expected, so their arrival caused a fair amount of anxiety among those present. My father, William— known to everyone as Bill—was not there at the time. When he received the news, his first thought was probably that he now had five children to feed and provide for.

At home in the village of Higham were my siblings: Dorothy, aged eleven; Janet, four; and Brian, two. They all lived in a small, terraced cottage on Church Street, which would now have to accommodate two new arrivals.

The cottage was one of a block of six similar dwellings, ours being at the end. That end wall had suffered structural damage and was "temporarily" supported by two steel plates fixed diagonally across it, forming an unsightly cross. Over the years, the plates had become rusted and corroded, making the building look rather dangerous.

Inside, the house was basic. There was a scullery at the rear and a front room with a door opening directly onto Church Street. Fresh water came from a single tap mounted on a standpipe in the centre of the block at the rear, shared by all six households.

Sewage drained into a cess pit at the end of the garden, which was emptied by tanker when it became full. The pit had no cover and was completely exposed, so anyone passing nearby had to be careful not to fall in. Our outdoor lavatory was located only about three yards away.

I did fall into the cess pit on one occasion. Luckily, my sister Janet managed to grab hold of my hair and shout for help. I could easily have drowned in that foul mess. After that incident, the farmer who owned the cottage made a wooden cover for the pit.

Each dwelling also had an outside outbuilding used for heating water. It was a brick structure containing an iron tub. Cold water had to be carried from the standpipe and poured in, then heated by lighting a fire underneath. This was done daily. All hot water for washing clothes and bathing came from this boiler and was scooped out with a large ladle into buckets, which were then carried into the scullery.

Bath time involved a portable tin bath placed on the scullery floor. Everyone in the family took turns using the same water. Naturally, the last person had the "pleasure" of a cooler bath, and the water had certainly seen better days. We all wanted to go first, but Mum made sure the order was strictly controlled so everyone had a fair turn.

When Mum finally came home with the two of us, Peter and I were put to sleep in wooden drawers removed from the chest of drawers in my parents' bedroom. The house was only suitable for a very small family—perhaps three people— but now there were seven of us. Space was tight, to say the least. Still, we managed. Peter and I were too young to notice any hardship. If we were fed, watered, and had our nappies changed, nothing else mattered.

Some of my earliest memories are of hiding under the large wooden table in the scullery during air raids. My mother would stand at the back door while German bombers flew overhead on their way to bomb the London docks, about twenty miles away. We were not a direct target, but bombs sometimes fell nearby, which was terrifying.

Barrage balloons floated above us, intended to prevent Stuka dive bombers from flying low enough to attack the nearby railway lines. They were tethered by long cables and seemed to fill the sky.

I also remember the V1 flying bombs—"doodlebugs," as they were known. They were especially frightening because they flew much lower than the bombers and usually came alone. They made a distinctive *phut-phut* sound, like a small two-stroke engine. When that sound stopped, you knew the engine had cut out and the bomb was about to fall. That was the moment to run for cover.

Unlike bombing raids, which were preceded by the wailing rise-and-fall of the air-raid sirens, doodlebugs gave little warning. That siren sound, dreadful as it was, frightened me almost as much as the bombers themselves.

For a time early in the war, I was cared for by William and Edith Slater, who lived in a bungalow close to the railway line. At the bottom of their garden, an air-raid shelter had been dug into the embankment. Whenever the siren sounded, we ran straight there and sometimes stayed all day and night if the bombing continued, which it often did.

The shelter made me feel safe—far more so than huddling under the table at home. There, I always felt vulnerable. I wanted my mother to leave the door and come and sit with us, but she never did. She stood watching the night sky as the anti-aircraft guns fired at the bombers. From under the table, I could see tracer bullets ripping glowing paths through the darkness. It was exciting and frightening at the same time—a strange and unforgettable contradiction.

William and Edith—Uncle Bill and Nan-Nan to me—were gentle, loving people. They had no children of their own and seemed to enjoy having a youngster in the house. Their garden was full of flowers and vegetables, and there was always enough to eat. Sometimes Nan would make custard and pour it over fresh raspberries from the garden. It felt like heaven.

Uncle Bill taught me to read and write. By the age of three, I could tell the time on the clock on the mantelpiece. He would sit me in a small chair by the log fire, move the hands around, and ask me what time it was. If I got it wrong—and I often did—he would patiently go over it again until it sank in.

He had shelves full of books and let me read any of them I wanted, regardless of the subject. He encouraged me simply to read—and read—and read. I will always be grateful to both for the love and attention they gave me during those early years.

At the age of five, I started at Higham Primary School. On my first morning, standing assembled in the playground, I was so frightened that I soiled my underpants. My sister Janet was sent home with me so I could change.

I remember the milk delivered to the school in crates of small bottles. In winter, the milk was sometimes frozen at the top, but we were expected to drink it regardless. Miss Nash was fearsome. She made us eat cabbage, swede, and an awful, powdered potato we called POM. I disliked her intensely at the time, though in fairness she was only doing her job.

The headmaster, Mr Nichols, was a kind and gentle man. In summer, he would take us around his garden and explain the plants to us. On Fridays, if we were lucky, there was a film show using an old 8mm projector. *Felix the Cat* was my favourite.

Mrs Nichols—his wife—was a different matter altogether. Loud and quick to shout, she frightened the life out of me on more than one occasion. Still, despite everything, there were happy times during those early years.

Summer Holidays

During the summer holidays, my mum would take us into the fields to help with pea picking, fruit picking, and whatever else was in season. There were always plenty of other children there as well, all pitching in. For us kids, it hardly felt like work at all. One of the great treats was riding on the horse-drawn carts through the orchards and across the fields. That alone made the day worthwhile.

In those days there was very little mechanisation on the farms. Everything was labour-intensive. Fields were often ploughed using a pair of Clydesdale horses—huge, powerful animals with a calm and gentle nature. You rarely see them now, except perhaps at a pageant or special event. Back then, animals were everywhere, and as children we would often help the farmers herd them into pens.

Children today are not allowed to do many of the things we did without a second thought. We're told it's all because of "health and safety." My opinion—for what it's worth—is rubbish.

During our childhood, mothers and children would arrive at the village station on steam trains from Strood and Gravesend. They came with their perambulators, babies tucked inside and spent the day working on the farms. If they were lucky, they might earn as much as fifteen shillings—seventy-five pence in today's money—for a full day of hard labour, before catching the train home again in the evening.

The perambulators had a second, unofficial purpose. They weren't just for babies. These sturdy old "chariots" were ideal for hiding the day's harvest— apples, pears, plums, peas, greengages, carrots, potatoes, cabbages, cauliflowers, or whatever else had been picked. The idea was to take the produce back into town and either sell it or give it to friends and neighbours.

I remember one occasion when the local policeman—Bobby Ward—was standing outside our house with a couple of the farmers' full-time workers, searching the perambulators. It was astonishing how many kilos of apples could be hidden beneath a baby. Those prams were nothing like the lightweight ones you see today. Many had false bottoms beneath the mattress, creating a surprisingly large storage space for what was politely called "stolen fruit."

Being caught with "swag" could be hard on the women involved. If a farmer caught them, they would usually be barred from working for him again. Still, there were several farmers in the village, and if one closed the door, another might be willing to take them on. Occasionally a farmer might pursue the matter further, but that rarely seemed to happen.

Sometimes my mum would send me home to fetch hot tea. I would go back to our house, make the tea with milk and sugar already mixed in, and pour it into a couple of empty milk bottles. I'd stuff newspaper into the tops to stop the tea spilling, then run all the way back to the field or orchard.

If the distance was long, the tea would be lukewarm—or even cold—by the time I arrived. When that happened, I would gather some twigs and dry grass, light a small fire, and heat the tea using a billy can. Once it was hot again, I'd pour it back into the bottles and hand them to my mum. It was all great fun, and we learned to take part and not take anything for granted.

As I grew older, Mum would give me pocket money at the end of the week. I received half a crown, which in today's terms is twelve and a half pence. With that, I could go to the cinema in the village hall and still have plenty left over. A ticket cost sixpence—a tanner, or two and a half pence in today's money—and I'd still have enough for a few sweets and other treats from the local grocery shop.

Grammar School

At the age of eleven, I was awarded a scholarship. This meant that I would begin my secondary education at the County Grammar School for Boys in Denton.

None of the children from my year went to that school. Most of the boys starting there already knew someone—perhaps a brother, cousin, or friend who was already a pupil. I knew no one at all. I was completely alone, and I felt it deeply.

Like all schools, it had its bullies and their victims. In a strange way, I have the bullies to thank—and this is why.

During my first few days, I became friends with a boy named Roy Robinson. Before long, he became the target of one of the school's most notorious bullies, a lad two years older than us both. His name was Perry—known to everyone as "Fat Perry" because of his size.

One day, as I walked into the quadrangle, Perry began shoving Roy about and slapping him across the face. I was frightened, but my fear quickly turned into anger. Without thinking, I launched myself at him.

It ended badly for both of us. Two prefects separated us and marched us straight to the headmaster. He gave us a lecture and singled me out as the instigator. I received "six of the best"—six strokes of the cane across the backside—and was sentenced to detention after school.

That evening, when I arrived at detention with the other so-called school villains, something unexpected happened. I was treated with respect for standing up to the school bully. That feeling—brief as it was—meant a great deal to me.

From that point on, however, I became something of a thorn in the side of the headmaster and many of the teachers. A couple of them I respected, but most struck me as snobbish. They made me feel inferior to boys whose parents were largely middle class.

In later years, I've accepted that part of the problem lay with me. I have always struggled at times with low self-esteem. These days I can usually get off the pity pot quickly, but as a boy I resented anyone who made me feel lesser because of my background. To be clear, my background was as good as anyone else's—it was my inferiority complex that caused most of my trouble.

One teacher in particular, Mr Light—known to us as "Dimmy"—seemed to take pleasure in humiliating me. One morning, he called me to the front of the class and questioned me aggressively about algebra, a subject I barely understood. He had already ridiculed me on previous occasions for my lack of knowledge.

That day, he told me to hold out my hands for the class to see. He then berated me for having dirty fingernails and demanded to know why.

I tried to explain. My mum worked in the fields and was often still out when I got home from school. We all had chores, and one of mine was to clean out the hearth and light the coal fire so we could have hot water and keep warm. That meant handling coal and ashes.

He mocked me. The class giggled. I was eleven years old, on the verge of tears, and utterly humiliated. Without thinking, I turned and ran out of the classroom. I could hear him shouting for me to come back, but I kept running—right the way home.

I stayed away from school for several days and didn't tell my mum. When the school eventually demanded a sick note, the truth came out and I was in trouble once again.

For much of my time at grammar school, detention became a regular feature of my life. Eventually, I found myself on what could only be described as indefinite detention.

One evening, I failed to turn up for detention. The next morning at assembly, my name was called and I was ordered to report to the headmaster. He asked why I hadn't attended. I gave him some excuse—probably a lie. I was caned again and given yet another detention.

That evening, I attended detention as ordered. When the roll was called, I answered, "Present, sir." A few names later, my name was called again. I replied once more, "Present, sir."

That was enough.

The following morning, I was summoned to the headmaster yet again. I received six more strokes for having "double detention." Apparently, double detention carried its own punishment, and because one of the detentions hadn't technically been served, it rolled over to the next day. These rules were devised by adults, yet somehow it was the children who were expected to understand them.

I realised then that I couldn't win. So, I stopped attending detention altogether. Instead, I took my punishment every morning—six of the best—until the end of term.

The following term, I was ordered to attend school on Saturday mornings to help the groundsman mark out rugby pitches and cut grass. Eventually, my dad discovered what was going on, promised nuclear retaliation, and that was the end of that.

Despite everything, it wasn't all bad. I was a poor student academically, often near the bottom of the class, and homework was something I regularly avoided. But I did well in rugby and cricket and was selected to play for the school teams in both sports.

Academically, I showed some ability in biology and art, but little else.

When I was about thirteen, I had a serious bicycle accident. A friend, Roy Gomme, had loaned me his bike, and I came off it badly. Although I was only hospitalised for two days, I had to attend the hospital daily for five or six weeks for injections and wound care.

At first, an ambulance collected me, but after a few days I had to travel by bus. I had skidded along the road face-first, and the right side of my face took most of the damage. A large scab formed, and I was eventually told I couldn't keep it covered.

I was mortified. I remember hating those journeys to and from the hospital, convinced that everyone was staring at me.

When I finally returned to school, I was so far behind that I couldn't catch up. My exam results were dreadful. At the start of the next school year, I was told I would have to repeat the year. Academically, it made sense—but emotionally, I was devastated.

I was now older than the rest of the class, surrounded by boys a year younger than me. I felt humiliated, alienated, and rebellious. I stopped caring. Truancy became normal, and I paid little attention to the consequences.

Around this time, I became involved in amateur boxing after a street fight with a rival gang. Although I lived in a village, there were boundaries. We had Lower Higham, where I was raised, and Upper Higham, where we moved to a council house in 1947. By twelve, I was firmly an Upper Higham lad, and former friends from Lower Higham had become *"the other lot"* —bloody silly, really.

Fights between the two groups were common. During one such fight, a boy from the Lower Higham gang and I were singled out by our local policeman, Mr Joe Barker.

In those days, every village had its own *"Bobby"*, and he lived among the people. They didn't hesitate to give a clip round the ear if you stepped out of line. It did us no harm, and parents accepted it as part of the system.

Joe told us to meet him the following evening at the Working Men's Club on Hermitage Road.

Boys' Club and Boxing

When we arrived, Joe had set up a makeshift boxing ring in the large hall. He put gloves on us both and told us to fight. I came off the better, and the other lad quit. That evening marked the beginning of what became the *Higham Boys' Club.*

Joe Barker was instrumental in its formation and was a wonderful man. I owe him a great deal, as do many others.

I trained regularly at the club, sparring with older lads. Because conscription was still in force, many young men had learned to box in the Army and were keen to pass on their knowledge.

One day, after I'd been absent from school for several days, I returned to discover my name had been entered to represent the school in an ABA schools boxing tournament. At the venue, my opponent was pointed out to me in the dressing room. His name was *Trevor Fish*. He looked skinny—much like me—and I assumed he would be no trouble.

I was wrong.

He completely outclassed me. All I remember are his gloves in my face, round after round. He wasn't hurting me so much as humiliating me. I barely landed a punch. The referee stopped the fight in the third round to save me from further punishment.

A few days later, on the bus home from school, a man spoke to me. He was a teacher at the Gordon School and ran their boxing team. Trevor Fish was one of his boys. He asked if I'd like to train with them. I agreed, and that was my introduction to proper boxing under the *Marquess of Queensberry rules.*

Truth be told, I was a better street fighter than a boxer and never achieved anything significant in my short amateur career. Trevor Fish, on the other hand, went on to become an *ABA champion* and later turned professional.

During the summer holidays of my third year at grammar school, I found work in a machine shop producing components for industry. I took to the work quickly, and within weeks I was setting up machine tools—capstan lathes, boring machines, and gear-cutting machines.

I clearly had an aptitude for it, and the owner asked if I would consider working for him when I left school. I told him my dad was keen for me to finish grammar school and hoped I might even get into Cambridge University. Many pupils from our school did go on to *Oxford or Cambridge,* and at that time a university education was considered a great privilege.

My Dad (William - (Bill)

He was born in Irlam in Lancashire on 2nd March 1898. As far as I know he had just one brother who was 3 years older than my dad. Their father was a coal merchant on a small scale who supplied the local community with coal. I don't know anything about his mother (my grandmother).

My dad developed rheumatic fever as an infant which led to a malady called *St. Vitus's Dance* in early childhood. This prevented him from receiving any schooling or any kind of formal education.

I later came to understand why it must have been hard for him as he watched one of his sons - (me), seemingly throwing away opportunities that in his eyes were invaluable.

Although he loved us all I believe that my rebellious nature became a wedge between us, and he came to favour my brother Alan rather than me. Now let me be clear these are not "sour grapes" I make no excuse for the way I developed as a youngster.

I could be difficult to handle and gave my mum and dad more stress that all the other kids combined. That is a fact.

But my dad loved me and never once in my life did he lay a hand on me, (although I certainly deserved it many times).

He would present arguments to me that were so honest and full of common down-to-earth sense that I never once won an argument against him.

And I mean NEVER - no matter what.

I learned so much from this wonderful man but never truly appreciated him until after he died.

At 11 years of age my dad got a job with a local butcher in the village of Irlam. My dad learned to slaughter animals such as pigs, sheep, and cattle. He was just 11 years old and did a man's work.

On Fridays, he would be working up until 10 or 11 o'clock at night to serve the needs of the men coming out of the pubs and wanting to take meat home to their families. This was how it was in the early 1900's. Remember, he was 11 years old when he started this.

In 1914, the Fist World War broke out and my dad enlisted. He took the *"Kings Shilling"*

It was *"Kitchener's Army"* and there were recruiting drives all over our country. For young men in those days that were not in uniform, the propaganda against them was awful.

My dad told me that the women in the street would harangue any man who was not in uniform and looked old enough to be wearing one.

At 16 and because he had matured quickly my dad looked a lot older and in fact did receive this disgusting treatment. You could say he hardly had a proper childhood.

When he joined the queue to sign up and take the *"Kings Shilling"* he was asked his age. When he replied *"17 sir"* he was told to come back when he was 18.

So, he joined another queue and told the officer he was 18. (he was in fact just 16 years old at the time)

After a very short basic training period my dad was shipped out to France and later to the Dardanelles for the campaign against Turkey.

It was the scene of some of the fiercest fighting of the war. Allied troops landed there in April 1915 and spent months on the small peninsula of land guarding the Dardanelles Straits in modern-day Turkey. The military aims of the campaign were not achieved and it was eventually called to a halt; the final Allied troops were evacuated in January 1916.

There were heavy casualties, not only from the fighting, but from the extremely unsanitary conditions. Of the estimated 213,000 British casualties, 145,000 were from illness. Surviving combatants also recalled the terrible problems with intense heat, swarms of flies, body lice, severe lack of water and insufficient supplies.

My dad looked after a mule train pulling supplies through the mud and the slush. He had a team of eight mules to pull the wagons or the cannons through the battlefields. He loved animals even though he had slaughtered so many as a young butcher in Irlam.

One afternoon a German shell exploded in front of the mules. Some were blown to pieces and my dad received shrapnel in the legs.

He told us he was catapulted off the carriage the carriage and ended up lying in the mud.

He could hear the screams of the injured and dying animals and was able to shoot two of the mules that were badly injured.

The next thing he knew was waking up in the battlefield hospital. He was there for a short time and after receiving treatment he was shipped back to Liverpool on a troopship, where he faced a disciplinary committee because he had lied about his age when he joined up.

He was discharged from the army but received no commendation for his courage or his patriotism. (I think this treatment of my dad and many others like him may have triggered the development of my often-cynical nature when it comes to matters related to *"the establishment"* or *"officialdom"*). My dad used to drink a lot but *was not* an alcoholic. He had a tremendous capacity for beer, and I once witnessed him taking up a beer drinking challenge from a contractor by the name of *Sid Todd*.

Now Sid, - (Toddy as he was called), was well known in the Medway area and had a reputation as a heavy drinker.

In those days, it was something of a *"claim to fame"* for a man to be able to consume gallons of the "amber nectar". He was always to be found in the Working Men's Club or the Three Crutches pub in Higham.

Anyway, my dad accepted the challenge provided that the one who gave up first would pay for all the beer consumed.

My dad won –drinking 17 pints of beer in the evening against Sid's 16 pints. It was a talking point in the pubs and clubs for several years after.

Sid had to be taken home, but my dad walked with me at his side from the club to our house in Taylors Lane. I was so proud of my dad.

I want to make one thing clear about my dad's drinking. He never ever kept us short because of it.

We came first and his drinking was financed by what he did *"on the side"*. He was a bit of a *"wheeler dealer"* and was very street wise. He was also quite lucky on the slot machines. He would watch people for hours playing these machines and had a gift of predicting approximately when a jackpot was due. He would then go to the machine with a handful of "tanners"- (old six-penny pieces) and invariably would win. I saw him do this several times. He was a shrewd old guy. One fellow I knew said to me once *"How does your dad do it, he is so lucky?"* I told him that it wasn't entirely luck. He calculated the odds. He never went to a machine without first studying what was happening beforehand.

My dad always smoked a pipe – never cigarettes. His tobacco was *"Condor-Twist"* - a very strong tobacco. He used to let my younger brother Alan and I have a puff on the pipe now and again, but it would always burn my tongue.

He did this in the hope of deterring us from smoking, but Alan and I ended up smoking cigarettes regularly from early on – about 12 or 13 years of age.

In fact, I never met anyone in my life who smoked more than I did. By the time I was about 37 old I was smoking 100 cigarettes a day. But I was living in Kuwait at this time and a carton of 200 Benson & Hedges King size filter cigarettes cost about £2.00 at the time. Today, as I write, those 200 cigarettes would cost £155.00 (yes about fifteen pounds and fifty pence for a pack of twenty).

I never realised this until June told me that she would buy for me a carton of 200 Marlborough cigarettes, or 200 Benson & Hedges King size filter every 2 days. I was living in Kuwait where cigarettes were very cheap at that time. I was earning a high salary and never really felt the effects of the monetary layout.

I had no idea. I just had a cigarette on all the time. I would light one cigarette from another much of the time. But that's another story.

Anyway, I don't know very much more about my dad's family because I was born and raised in Kent and we never met any of his family or the family of my mum.

My dad had only 8 or 9 months of schooling in his entire life as he suffered from an illness called St Vitus Dance when he was a boy.

He had to work full time from the age of 11 and was fighting on the front-line during World War 1.

So, when I was offered the opportunity of a good education, he wanted me to take that opportunity.

I can understand that today but then I just thought he was being unreasonable when he said that there were better things ahead for me.

I cajoled my mum to have a go at my dad and let me go to work for the man who owned the engineering machine shop. Eventually she persuaded him, and we obtained exceptional permission from the school so that I could leave school on my 15th birthday which was the very same day that the next academic year was to commence. So, in fact, I started full time work at fourteen years of age.

I was over the moon with this and from then on, I became a real pain in the butt to everyone at home as I considered I was now a REAL working man.

I must be honest and say that the school authority did not object one bit even though my dad had previously agreed for me to continue at the Grammar School until I reached the age of 18. You may draw your own conclusions if you wish.

After I had been working at the machine shop for about 7 months or so my dad got me an interview with the HR section at a factory owned by the Birfield Group of companies. I was offered a student apprenticeship that was designed to groom me for an eventual management position within the group.

He was so happy when I accepted to take this offer even though the money offered was only about 30% of what I was earning at the machine shop.

I recall very clearly the personnel manager telling me that my starting wage would be one pound sixteen shillings and eleven pence three farthings per week, but....... this would increase after I signed the indentures which could only be done after my 16th birthday. I agreed to this and after giving my current employer a weeks' notice I started work at the Birfield Group.

It wasn't too long before I knew in my heart that I could not be doing this for the rest of my life. I was unfairly judging those good people that were working in the factory and although I never said so I thought they were on a hiding to nothing and what was good enough for them was not ever going to be good enough for me.
It's not that I had any ambition or had set any kind of target for myself, but I just knew that I could not be getting up every morning and going to the same place to work every morning and coming home every evening year in year out for the rest of my life.

As it happened my pal Tony Taylor had made some inquiries about attending a Sea Training School and then go to sea after the training was over. He was a bit nervous about it as he was told it was a tough course. When we discussed it, he suggested we both apply and go together, and we could support each other if the going got rough. This sounded like a good idea, and I agreed.

After we had done the groundwork and knew the process we had to take, I told my mum about it. She didn't like the idea and said my dad would never agree to sign the necessary paperwork.
I again put on the charm with my mum and eventually my dad relented. He told me in no uncertain terms what he thought of merchant seamen, (***"the scum of the earth"*** he called them), but I was absolutely delighted that he had agreed to sign the paperwork.
My dad passed away on 20th May 1981 in his 84th year.

My Mum

She was born and raised in Yorkshire in a village outside of Redcar. She would often talk lovingly about the hills and dales of Yorkshire.
Like my father, she never lost her northern accent even though she never went back to her beloved county. She was tall and slim and quite pretty with a mop of pure white hair which made her stand out in any crowd.
In her early years she worked in the fashion industry as a "mannequin" as they called the girls who modelled the clothes in those days.
I don't know how or when she met my dad, but I do know she was married earlier to another man who was cruel to her, and she was taken away from him by my dad. That's all I know at the time of writing or will probably ever know.

She had six of us, (4 boys -2 girls). Except for my eldest sister Dorothy (who was born in Swindon), and Janet in Greenwich, the rest of us were born in Kent. Mum lost two of her children as I have explained earlier.

Most of her life she worked to keep us in shoes and clothes because the wages of my dad hardly went anywhere near to make life comfortable.

In those days, it was so different from today, (not just for us but for most families as I remember).

She was liked by most people who knew her. She was kind natured and loved to laugh. She had a great sense of humour.

I remember the time when her false breast fell from her bra whilst she bent down in the kitchen to pick something up from the floor. The false breast was just a bag of beads really, and it plopped into the bucket of water.

I just reached into the bucket and picked up the bag and said something like "you dropped your boob mum" and we both roared with laughter. I was in fact expecting her to maybe shed a tear or two but not my mum. She just got on with things.

My mum developed a cancer and had mastectomy surgery performed when she was about 53 and, in those days, it was not uncommon to face the knife.

Although my dad never laid a finger on me and just once to my brother Alan, that was not the case for my mum. She would whack us with a stick if we went too far and we often got it across the legs or the backside.

To be honest, I used to pretend it didn't hurt just to wind her up which made her even angrier.

But all in all, it was not uncommon in those days for a parent to dish out this kind of punishment and it was common in the schools.

In my personal experience this kind of punishment did not have long lasting effects on either myself or Alan.

But then, I can only speak for myself and not for others - who may have an entirely different point of view.

When we were out of order excessively, we got a clout for it if we did not pack it in.

I am not saying that I advocate child corporal punishment in the world we live in today, but I do think a lot of nonsense is provided to the media and elsewhere about the effects of it.

I am not talking about sadistic punishment but just a smack across the backside or the legs for example. But nowadays if I aired such sentiments or comments in public I might be vilified. But I am used to speaking my mind and if anyone is offended, be assured my opinions are not intended to offend. I'm just saying what I think, that's all.

I never had to smack my own son for anything in his life, but it doesn't mean to say I would never have done so if there was no alternative.

I also will **not condemn** someone else for smacking (in moderation) their own children in certain circumstances. **Who am I to judge others?** Anyway, enough said about this............

Because my mum worked in the fields most of the year including wintertime I would come home from school to an empty house. My eldest sister was now married and lived in London and my sister Janet was now working.

My first job in the winter months would be to clean out the fire grate and prepare a new fire to get some warmth in the house.
In those days, council houses were built without insulation. There was no such thing as double glazing for council dwellers in those days. They were like *"ice boxes"* in fact and in the winter, ice would form on the inside of the windows.

Our heating system was a coal fire in the *"front room"*, and woe betide anyone who came in or out of the room and left the door open. The heat would leave the room quickly and we would all huddle around the fire on very cold days and nights. And I remember that every time the door to the room opened for entry or exit, there would be a back draft from the chimney, and we would all get a taste of smoke billowing into the room if the fire was not glowing red.

Today, people bang on about pollution killing our youngsters, but our generation had so much pollution to contend with and we live to tell the tale. *(As I put this on paper, I'm in my 85th year).*

I'm not saying we should not take care of our environment, we most certainly should, but I do think some of our "experts" talk a lot of tripe at times.

Anyway, after getting the fire lit, the next thing to do would be to peel the potatoes and prepare the vegetables. I would place them ready for mum to prepare when she came home – usually before 6:00pm.
Then she would get dinner ready for us. My dad would not get home until about 8:30pm on each weekday but was earlier on Saturdays and Sundays.

When we were younger my brother and I would be in bed when he arrived home. He would sometimes come upstairs with a packet of Smiths crisps for us to share and we would pester him *to "tell us about when you were a boy dad"*.
This is how we learned things from him. Apart from the *"half day weekends"* we hardly saw him.
My Dad worked 7 days a week for as long as I can remember - even up to his 70th year when he retired on pension. My mum passed away on 13 March 1976 in her 75th year.

CHAPTER 2

Sea Training School

After Mum finally persuaded Dad to sign the paperwork for sea training school, I went straight to my mate Tony to tell him I was ready to go. That was when he dropped a bombshell—he'd changed his mind and decided not to go after all.

I was disappointed, but it made no difference. My mind was made up. I was accepted for training by the British Shipping Federation and sent to Sharpness, in Gloucestershire, to join the training ship *Vindicatrix*.

What a shock to the system that turned out to be.

When we stepped off the train from London at Sharpness station, we were met by a group of lads from the training ship under the command of an officer wearing Merchant Navy uniform. The lads were dressed in pea jackets and wide-bottomed trousers—the standard uniform for recruits. It wasn't long before I was wearing the same outfit, which, to my eye, was utterly unattractive.

This was the 1950s, and boys my age dressed very differently. We favoured the Edwardian look—long jackets almost to the knees with velvet collars and cuffs, skin-tight drainpipe trousers with three-inch turn-ups, chucka boots, and brightly coloured socks. Most of us wore our hair long. Mine was shoulder-length and, as black as your hat.

Our musical heroes were Bill Haley, Elvis Presley, Buddy Holly, Tommy Steele and others of that era.

Now, suddenly, we were being shouted at by boys not much older than ourselves.

We were marched about a mile up the road carrying heavy kit bags that we'd all been required to buy beforehand. As we approached the top of a rise, we saw a cluster of Nissan huts inside a compound surrounded by high wire fencing. As we passed through the gates, we could see boys standing in groups on the parade ground. Officers were shouting and swearing, and my stomach churned.

I remember thinking: *What on earth have I let myself in for?*

At one point, two boys in our column turned around and bolted back through the gates towards the station. No one stopped them. They received a few jeers and catcalls, but that was all. The rest of us said nothing. I think most of us were in shock. I know I was.

We were made to stand in line for what felt like an eternity before a man named **Mr Adegate** addressed us. He made it very clear that from that moment on, we would do exactly as we were told.

There were about twenty-six of us—**"New Boys"**—from all over the country. Some came from the Gorbals in Glasgow, others from Dingle in Liverpool, Cardiff, Huddersfield, Aberdeen, Hartlepool, and places I'd never even heard of. The accents were thick and unfamiliar, and I often struggled to understand what was being said.

I was the only boy from south-east England and once again felt isolated. Before long, though, I became friendly with a lad from Huddersfield who was also the only one from his area. We shared that sense of being outsiders.

We were marched off to a Nissan hut that would be our billet for the first six weeks. After that, we'd move aboard the training ship for the remainder of our stay.

Uniforms were issued—pea jackets, wide-bottomed trousers, boots, oilskins, and other gear. We hated it. But this was part of the process. Individuality was to be stripped away and replaced with uniformity. At the time, we resisted it fiercely. Years later, I came to understand that it was necessary—and a powerful builder of character. I wouldn't have admitted that back then, but with age came gratitude for the toughness we were subjected to.

All the huts were heated by coal-burning stoves with steel chimneys poking through the roofs. Coal was delivered weekly and dumped in a heap in one of the open areas of the camp. One day, I was caught fighting with a boy from Glasgow who regularly gave me grief whenever his mates were around. I caught him on his own, and we had a scrap.

Our punishment was unusual. We were ordered to first gather fifty pieces of coal from the coal bunker. After washing them with water, we were made to whitewash every lump and stack them neatly. Naturally, we were mercilessly mocked by the other lads. It took several days of this before the officer decided we'd been punished enough.

All of this was done in our own time after normal training hours. We'd work until we were sent to the ablutions to wash the coal dust from our bodies.

The ablution huts were basic, just rows of lavatories on one side, wash basins on the other. There were no showers.

We stripped naked, stood in line, and washed ourselves with cold water and a bar of soap. If anyone took too long, one of the instructors would walk down the line and slap our bare buttocks with a slipper. Looking back, I'm sure one or two of them took a bit too much pleasure in that.

After washing, we dressed, returned to the billet, and ten minutes later the lights went out. It wasn't pleasant, but oddly enough, it brought my adversary and me closer together. After that episode, we became good friends.

Another misdemeanour landed me scrubbing the wooden 'tween deck. Scrubbing decks was routine, but this time I was given only a bucket and a nailbrush and assigned a specific area. It bred resentment toward the officers but strengthened bonds with others who were suffering similar treatment.

At the time, it hurt. In later years, the psychology behind it all became clear. Now, I can look back and laugh. It did me no harm at all. In fact, it taught me that I was not the centre of the universe—and that it was fine to be just another *"bozo on the bus"*, provided I retained my dignity as an *"individual bozo"* with choices to make.

My time at the training ship changed my outlook on life. Growing up in a village in Kent, I'd been sheltered from many realities. Here, regional identities mattered. To most northerners, I was *"the Cockney."* Welsh boys were *"Taffy,"* Scots were *"Jock,"* Liverpudlians were *"Scouse,"* from Birmingham came the *brummies''* and lads from Tyneside were *Geordies.*

Most boys stuck with others from their own region. Those of us without local allies banded together. There were plenty of fights, usually settled during shore leave in the nearby town of Berkeley. I had several such encounters, always one-on-one. There was a code. Ganging up on one individual simply wasn't done.

We had no money for drink or drugs even if we'd wanted them. We received five shillings—twenty-five pence—a week, which had to cover everything except food and laundry. We bought rolling tobacco and cut matches in half lengthwise with a razor blade to make them last longer.

The food was basic, and we were always hungry. If anyone received a food parcel from home, it was shared by everyone in the billet. No one hoarded. If one lad had a single cigarette and the rest had none, it was passed around so everyone got a puff. That was how it was. We really were all in the same boat.

I remember our first meal clearly. It was Monday evening. The mess deck had long wooden tables with benches, seating ten boys to a table. In the middle of each table was a plate of sliced bread—eleven slices.

The extra slice was prized. It went to the boy who drew the number eleven written on pieces of cardboard in a bag..

We queued by table at the galley and were served one ladle of the evening's offering—Sea Pie. It was a baked mixture of leftovers from the previous day. We all swore we'd never eat such rubbish and gladly gave our portions to boys at other tables who asked for them.

Within a week, we were begging New Boys for their Sea Pie. Monday nights became our favourite meal of the week because it offered the chance of a double helping. Despite constant hunger, every one of us gained weight by the time we left. Whether that was down to the food or creative use of the scales, I'll never know.

Eventually, passing-out day arrived. We marched to the station wearing uniforms we were now proud of. The Teddy Boy mindset had gone. I was excited—eager to go to sea on my first voyage.

Coming home was something of a let-down. I'd imagined a hero's welcome. Instead, my mates teased me mercilessly about the uniform. Within days, the long jacket and drainpipe trousers were back on, and I was one of the boys again rather than a *"peanut,"* as I'd been called.

But something had changed. I now felt a strong pull to see the world—to discover things I knew I'd never find by staying in Kent. I was ready to fly.

CHAPTER 3 My Sea Career

After I'd been home for a few days, a telegram arrived from the Shipping Master at the Shipping Federation. I was instructed to report with my gear to the Dock Street office in South London.

When I arrived, I went through the usual medical examination and was then told to report to the master of a tanker called **British Hero**. She was berthed at the Isle of Grain refinery in Kent. The moment I stepped aboard I was stunned by her size. To me she was enormous—though in those days a 16,000-ton ship was considered only intermediate. The big tankers of that period were nearer 28,000 tons.

I was shown to my cabin in the stern, below decks. It was spacious, with plenty of storage, and—best of all—I had it to myself. I knew that on many other types of ship, especially passenger vessels and general cargo ships, cabins like that could be shared by four, six, even eight men. But **British Hero** was an oil tanker owned by British Petroleum (BP), and I felt I'd landed on my feet.

An officer took me to the lower bridge deck to sign on in the presence of the Master and the Shipping Master representing the Federation. I signed on as a **Deck Boy** at a wage of **£11 15s a month**. Yes—per month. I was expected to work **seven days a week**, and if I was required to work extra time I would be paid **1s 8d an hour**.

I arranged for **£5 a month** to be deducted and sent to Mum. She had worked in the fields to help cover the costs of my training. The training itself was "free," but there were plenty of associated expenses that the trainees paid for. Even our five shillings a week pocket money at training school had come from our parents, not from the Federation.

Back in my cabin, a sailor came to take me to meet my new boss—the *boatswain*.

He was a stocky Aberdonian called **Alan Scott**, the ship's bosun. From the first moment I met him I knew there'd be no messing about. He had the look of a man who meant what he said and said exactly what he meant.

He took me on a brisk tour and explained my duties—one compartment at a time.

First the **sailors' messroom**: my responsibility. Then the **sailors' bathrooms and toilets**: Then the **recreation room**. Then the **petty officers' messroom**. Then the **petty officers' bathrooms and toilets**. Then the **alleyways and companionways** (the staircases) connecting them all.

Every one of those areas had to be cleaned properly every morning **before 11:00 a.m.** And he meant properly.

Then came the catering side of it. I was to collect the food from the galley, where it was prepared in kits, and place it into the bain-maries in each messroom. I also had to keep both messrooms supplied with fresh tea and coffee—**seven times a day**: at seven bells in the morning watch, then at 08:00, 10:30, 12:00, 14:30, 17:00, and finally 20:00. Only after that could I rest.

Between those set times, everything else still had to be done.

At first I assumed I'd be given help. Two or three assistants at least. I was dreaming. It was **me, and me alone**, and I had to learn how to manage it.

It meant working all day. I was up at **4:00 a.m.**. After washing and dressing I got straight into it. For the first few weeks I barely had a minute to myself. I didn't even sit down to eat with the others. I'd shove food onto a plate, take mouthfuls while rushing between the poop deck and the messrooms, then run again.

I'm writing this now and it would be impossible for me to do even a fraction of it today—but back then I did it, and more. And the astonishing thing is **I loved it.**

I rarely felt exploited. The stick I got early on, I took as part of the learning curve. The crew and petty officers gave me a nickname: **"Peggy."** Not because of any effeminate tendencies—nothing of the sort. It came from the old sailing-ship days, when a man who'd lost a leg and been fitted with a peg-leg could no longer climb rigging or work the deck, so he was often put in the mess to look after the men. Hence: Peggy.

I didn't mind it at all. In fact, I earned a lot of respect from the crew because they appreciated the work I did on their behalf.

My working day was long—typically **4:15 a.m. to 8:00 p.m.** If we hit heavy weather at night and all hands had to turn out, I was expected to be up and moving like everyone else.

The only thing I truly hated was **bad weather**. In storms I was seasick—properly seasick, not a bit of queasiness. Every time the ship met heavy seas I'd go down, and it was dreadful.

Seasickness and the Indian Ocean

British Hero traded mainly between East African ports and Arabian Gulf ports, which meant we were often in the **Indian Ocean**. In certain months, the monsoons could turn that ocean into a fury. The ship could be thrown around like a cork.

In those storms I was utterly miserable. A serious bout of seasickness is as bad as anything I've ever suffered. Your head spins, your balance disappears, your heart races, you ache like you've got flu, and you feel weak to the bone. I'd cling to anything that could steady me and vomit uncontrollably. I couldn't work properly. In the worst spells I wanted only to lie down and die. Literally.

Most of the crew had some sympathy, but the bosun did not. Alan Scott believed in brute force remedies. If he found me in my bunk he would drag me out and roar at me to get on deck and *"face it."* He insisted I would never get over it otherwise.

It didn't work. I'd stand at the rail trying to look at the horizon—except one moment the horizon was above my head and the next it was below my feet. I can smile at it now, but I will never forget how awful it was.

Then came the turning point.

Every Sunday, as was customary in those days, the Master made his rounds with the Chief Officer, Chief Engineer and the bosun for the **Captain's Sunday Inspection**. One of my responsibilities was keeping the accommodation, messrooms, pantries, and ablutions clean and orderly.

One Sunday the Master looked at me closely and asked if I was ill. I said, *"No, sir—I'm fine today."* He told me I'd lost weight. The bosun piped up and said it was because I was regularly seasick and couldn't keep food down.

A week later, during inspection, the Master complained that the bain-marie in the sailors' pantry was unclean. He wore a white glove and sometimes ran it along surfaces as a test. He didn't rebuke me—he rebuked the **Chief Officer**. Naturally the Chief then tore into the bosun later.

After inspection the bosun found me and yelled that he was going to get me replaced. He yelled at somebody every day, so I didn't know what to think—but I was frightened he meant it.

That evening a midshipman came and told me to report to the Master immediately. I assumed I was in trouble and expected punishment. In those days, under the Merchant Shipping rules, a Master could stop money for what they called *"dereliction of duty."*

I knocked, was told to come in, and to my surprise the Master wasn't stern at all. He told me kindly without malice that he was arranging to pay me off in **Cape Town**, which we were then heading for.

I was devastated. I was sixteen years old and close to tears. I loved the sea life, even with everything that was battering me. He said it wasn't the inspection—he had good reports about my work from the Chief Officer and, to my surprise, even from the bosun. He said he was concerned for my health. Then he said something that stuck with me: that not everyone gets over seasickness, and *"maybe God has other plans for you"*.

I left his office in tears. I couldn't imagine life without the sea.

Then, the following Sunday, we hit truly bad weather—deep monsoon conditions. I prepared for inspection as usual and, unbelievably, I wasn't badly affected. The Master noticed. He asked if the weather was troubling me, and I told him the truth: I hadn't been seasick since the day he said he was going to pay me off.

To cut a long story short, he did **not** pay me off in Cape Town—and I was never seasick again in the way I had been before. It wouldn't be true to say I was never sick again, because on other ships I was, but I never again suffered those horrors for the rest of my sea service.

I've often wondered whether it was fear that caused the change, or something else entirely. It doesn't really matter. I just wanted to share it.

Learning the job

As the months passed, I grew more confident and persuaded the bosun to let me spend about an hour each afternoon on deck so I could develop proper seamanship skills.

I also managed to get one of the ABs to let me steer the ship in his place. Steering a tanker at sixteen years old was thrilling beyond words. I volunteered for lookout duty on the fo'c'sle head as well. I'd often turn in around 21:00, sleep a couple of hours, then get up and relieve the man on watch.

I loved the solitude at the bow—away from the throb of machinery at the other end of the ship. I'd watch porpoises riding the bow wave and marvel at the phosphorescence in the water. Sometimes I imagined the porpoises knew they were being watched and were performing especially for me—though of course they were simply enjoying the ride.

In those days, four- or five-hours' sleep seemed to be enough. Now? Well… that's another story.

Pay-Off and Reality

About **nine and a half months** later, after many ports of call, we docked in **South Shields** on the Tyne. We were paid off and I received my account for the voyage. The total for **9 months and 17 days** came to **£171 14s 2d**, including **37.5 days' paid leave**.

After deductions of **£112 2s 8d**, I took home **£59 11s 6d**.

I still have the original pay-off slip in my files. Looking at it now, the figures still astonish me. When you break it down, it works out to pennies a day, and a few pence an hour once you consider the hours worked. Hard to believe—yet it's true.

I paid off the ship, caught the train from Newcastle to London and then on to Kent. It was wonderful to be home, but my money didn't last long. Within days I was looking for another ship.

What still rankled was the overtime. I'd been told I would be paid for it, but I hadn't kept a proper log of my hours, and that was a lesson learned the hard way. Years later I discovered that working a boy rating those sorts of hours would have caused serious trouble if it had been officially examined. At the time, I didn't know any of that. I don't condone exploitation—but I can honestly say it didn't break me. The only real resentment I held was towards the officer who reassured me at the start and then—one way or another—the reality didn't match the promise.

More Ships, More Trouble

I continued sailing on a variety of ships over the next few years.

I remember being on a ship called *Varicella* during the **Cuban Missile Crisis** in 1962. In those days we didn't have wall-to-wall news. What we learned came from shortwave radio and slower channels—ship-to-ship messages, sometimes even Morse code with an Aldis lamp.

During that period, we were trading around the Caribbean, right where the tension was thickest. There was talk of Russian ships pushing on toward Cuba and threats flying back and forth. It was a tense time, and I wanted to get home. So, I jumped ship. This came after we left the Caribbean and headed for Rotterdam.

Unfortunately, my *"so-called girlfriend"* in Rotterdam shopped me to the police. I was arrested and put in a cell. The authorities contacted the ship and told me that if I agreed to return, the Master was willing to pay me off. That sounded fair enough, so I agreed.

When I got back aboard, it was a different story. The Master refused to pay me off and had me confined in the ship's hospital under guard. He was furious and told me he would have me charged with desertion when we reached the UK. I was shocked when he said our next port of call was UK. Had I known this before I would not have jumped ship.

C'est la vie, n'est-ce pas.

When we berthed in South Shields, the police came aboard. I was taken to the ship's office while the Master ranted in front of the police and Shipping Master.

He appeared to have been drinking again, and oddly enough that worked in my favour. After a long, heated discussion, it was decided I couldn't be charged with a civilian offence, but the Master could punish me under the Merchant Shipping rules and give me an unfavourable discharge.

In the end, my pay was forfeited—within the articles we'd signed, it could be done. All I was given was a railway warrant back to London.

I will say this: I'd been sailing with a decent crew, and they proved it. The lads had a whip-round, took me to the pub, and made sure I got on the train with a few pounds in my pocket.

I arrived home wide-eyed and legless.

Within days, I was off again—this time to West Africa on a Palm Line ship. By then I really was scraping the bottom of the barrel, but as the saying goes: beggars can't be choosers. In those days, I never saved real money. I thought bank accounts were for boring people who didn't know how to live.

In those years I began drinking heavily, and it often led me into trouble—with police, employers, family, friends, strangers, you name it. My relationships with women weren't rare, but they were nearly always short-lived.

I can't possibly list all the escapades here, but the truth is I enjoyed much of my time in the Merchant Navy. Most employers considered me a good worker—except when I started drinking. Then the drink took over, and I'd vanish.

Even early on, alcohol became a taker. It took girlfriends, jobs, licences, freedom, self-respect, friendships—more than I can easily list. And still I drank, each time believing I would "be okay this time."

I didn't understand then that I'd become an alcoholic at an early age.

Now I know what alcohol is: cunning, baffling, and powerful. Without help it was far too much for me. But I was strong-willed and stubborn, and I would never have believed I was powerless over "a drink or two."

And when I took a drink, the drink took me? No way. HOW WRONG I WAS.

CHAPTER 4

The Hod Carrier

During the time I was going to sea, I would sometimes pay off the ship and come home to mum and dad. After my money was spent, I would go and get another ship to sail.

It was easy enough in those days and there were not the restrictive practices that are found in today's world.

One time during 1960 I came home and met a girl I really liked. Her name was Maureen. I told my mum I had met a girl and said I think I will stay ashore for a while. She was so pleased and told me that they were looking for workers on the new house building site just across the road from our house in Taylors Lane, Higham.

And so, I walked onto the site and asked a worker where I could find the foreman. He told me to go to the hut up the road and ask for Fred Pinney.

When I found Fred Pinney, he said he was looking for Hod-Carriers. I had no idea even what a hod-carrier was, let alone what they did, but promptly told him I was indeed a hod-carrier.

"Can you start right away" he asked.

I said *"Yes, tomorrow morning".* And I went away happy.

On the way back to our house, I again spoke to the man who had told me where to find the foreman. He was about my age, and I asked him, *"What's a hod carrier?"*

He pointed to a fellow not far from us who was climbing a ladder with a metal box on his shoulder which had a short wooden staff attached to it. The hod was filled with 12 bricks.

I thought to myself, well it's not rocket science and I can surely do that. And so, the next morning I was introduced to Paddy, the man I was going to work alongside. He handed me a hod.

He knew immediately that I had no experience as a hod-carrier. But Paddy was a decent fellow and covered for me while I got the hang of it.

I got home the first day absolutely shattered and my right shoulder was blistered and bruised. My fingers were blistered and bleeding with picking up the bricks all day and placing them in the hod. I would sometimes pinch the tips of my fingers when placing the bricks after delivering them on the scaffold.

My mum wanted me to give it up right away, but I was determined to overcome the pain. I knew it would take time, but I was hungry for the job and I needed the money. This went on for about 7 or 8 days, and I eventually worked through the pain and became somewhat better than when I started.

After about 3-4 weeks I was able to keep up with any of the others and in fact could do more than any of them when I was racing.

It became a challenge for me to beat the best hoddie on the site. And in about 6 weeks there was not one hoddie on the site who could stay with me.

With my long legs I could place the ladder at an angle that would allow me to run up the ladder two rungs at a time - sometimes 3 rungs at a time depending on the situation.

Then instead of using the rungs on the descent, I would place my feet on the sides of the ladder and slide all the way down. This enabled me to load out between three thousand six hundred and four thousand bricks per day.

In those days, if a man became a good hoddie, the word got around the industry because it was all about money. The more a brick and mortar a hoddie could supply the brickie's, the bigger the bonus.

And so, the word got around about the *"hoddie from Higham"*.

One morning a man from Gravesend working with another gang of brickies came over to where we were building a pair of three-bedroom houses and challenged me to a competition.

This man was from the district known as *"Rats Island"* near Denton Wharf. It was a tough area and many of the people who lived there were travellers. His name was **Peter Ives,** and he had a formidable reputation as a scrapper and a hod-carrier.

Peter was much shorter than me but very powerfully built, and his reputation went before him. Many of the building workers on the site knew of him.

The challenge was accepted by me, and the site foreman allowed us to compete on his site.

The basis of the challenge entailed both of us working side by side loading out houses on the top lift.

This meant we each loaded our hods from the *same* stack on the ground and used separate ladders to climb to the top scaffold which was about 30cm below gutter height on a block of houses - (about 20 feet above ground level).

We began at 7:00 am one morning as arranged and it was established that the winner would be the first one who landed 5 hods more that his opponent.

We ran and ran and ran up and down those ladders until about 4 in the afternoon without a break except by mutual agreement for a smoke periodically.

But at 4:00 pm we were both very tired and Peter just looked at me and put out his hand. At this time, I was 2 hods ahead of him. He said he'd had enough and could do no more and congratulated me.

But to be the winner, I had to continue take a final 3 hods of bricks to the top which of course I did. There were lots of congratulations from many of the workers on the site who had been watching on and off our competition.

I know there were many side bets amongst the workforce, and I found out later that my foreman (Fred Pinney), had won quite a bit because he had bet on me beating Peter. I didn't know at the time, but he had previously worked with *Peter Ives* on another job and knew his abilities.

From that day on, I never had to ask for work - (as a hoddie that is).

It always came through people offering me work as **a hod-carrier/scaffolder**

I would leave a job in the middle of the week if someone offered me an extra sixpence an hour to go and work for them. It probably sounds disloyal to those who have not experienced those years but that is the way it was.

Many of us worked *"on the lump"* as it was known in those days. There was a construction boom going on and we would earn good money. I could earn more in just two days than my dad could earn in seven.

But although I paid my bills and was paying my way, apart from that I didn't save very much.

The girl that I had met - (Maureen), whom had been the reason for me becoming a hoddie, was a lovely girl from Herne Bay. Her dad was a friend of Edward Heath who later became UK Prime Minister.

But the yearning to get back to sea was too strong for me and one day I just packed in the job I was on and got another ship.

I didn't realise how much this upset the poor girl until later and my mum was mad at me. She really liked this lassie and so did I, but I was just so thoughtless. I just wanted my freedom and like I often would do I just ran away from responsibility.

And this was somewhat of a pattern with me for a while. I would go away for a few months on a ship. Come home, *"fall in love"* for a while and then clear off again. I know today that I was always looking for something in those years *but did not really know what it was I was looking for.*

Dreamland

After paying off a ship in the sixties, I took my mum and dad to Margate for a day out.

Whilst walking around in the funfair known as DREAMLAND, I got into conversation with a fellow called *Jack Pierce* who was working on one of the sideshows.

Jack had previously served in the Merchant Navy, and we hit it off swapping our seafaring adventures. He asked me if I would like to work on the stall with him as he needed another hand. It seemed like a great idea to me at the time and I agreed. I took mum and dad back home and the following day went off to Margate.

I met up with Jack and got myself some digs (bed and breakfast). The place I stayed was run by a nice lady and as I planned to stay for the whole season. she rented me a nice clean room at a very reasonable rate.

I quickly fell into the way of things at the job and enjoyed it very much. I was still in my late teens and there were plenty of girls visiting the park and I made several new friends.

We would work the stall until 11:00pm and then close. The park would then close until the following morning. After we closed the flash, we went to night-clubs, and this was our primary leisure time. We had one day off each week. It was great.

One day Jack proposed to me a scheme where we could set up a small nappy exchange business.

The idea was that we would convert the garage to his house in Margate and install some washing machines and dryers in there. Then we would have a couple of people to collect soiled nappies from the many households and immediately exchange them for freshly laundered ones. The soiled ones would be washed dried and ready for the next distribution. A girl Jack knew would be the laundress.

At first, I was enthusiastic as there was no other such service in Margate. But I began to have my doubts after doing a bit of research and some calculations and as it would mean that I would be committed to a loan from somewhere to set the operation up, I pulled out of the proposed deal.

Jack was disappointed in me, and this led to some friction between us.

Now Jack was someone you did not get on the wrong side of as I learned not just by his reputation but by seeing him in action.

His wife was a lovely girl called Heather and she was very attractive. But Jack was playing around with other women, and she tried to make him jealous by allowing a guy who was a professional snooker player to hang around and flirt with her.

This came to the attention of Jack who made it known that nobody flirts with his woman and gets away with it. I was in the club one night when Jack came in and went over to the snooker table where this guy was playing.

I watched Jack hit the fellow on the back of the head with a snooker ball. The guy fell onto the table and Jack took his snooker cue, broke it in two pieces over his knee and smashed the fingers of the snooker player with the broken cue.

The poor fellow was in agony as Jack took his other hand and smashed the cue over the other fingers.

No-one tried to stop him, and I found out later that this had put an end to the snooker player's career.

So, when I say it was not a good idea to get on the wrong side of Jack Pierce then perhaps you can see why.

As it was coming to the end of the season, I decided to disappear from the scene and left Margate without telling anyone and shipped out again. I never saw Jack again and thought it wise not to go down to Margate for a while in case I ran into him or his brother.

1961

It was Christmas Eve in 1961 and I was working on a building site in Cliffe.

My boss was Joe Edwards, a bear of a man about 18 stone with hands like shovels.

Joe was a subcontractor for mainly brickworks, and this was one of his projects. I was his hoddie and there were 3 other bricklayers in the gang.

At lunchtime we decided to go to The Bells - a pub in the village. We all agreed to just have a Christmas drink together - (just a couple of pints each) and then return to the site and finish the work.

Well, we have all heard about the best laid plans of mice and men have we not?

And after we were beginning to enjoy ourselves, a fellow came into the pub and told us he had a lorryload of fletton bricks for us.

I went outside and sure enough there was the lorry with 5500 bricks.

In my slightly drunk condition, I thought it would be a great joke to offload the bricks at the kerbside around the corner from the pub.

And that's what I started to do until I was rudely interrupted by the lorry driver and Joe who certainly didn't see the funny side of it, and they became very angry with me.

Joe went for me and we started fighting in the street. Anyway, I caught him a beauty and he ended up with a broken nose.

This all led to me being fired and I went back into the pub whilst the bricks were loaded back into the lorry, and Ralph was taken to the hospital to get his nose straightened out.

I eventually got home to my mum's house later and went for a nap.

When I woke up, I went downstairs, and my mum asked me where my working bag was with my vacuum flask.

I had left them at the site, and she understandably began to chastise me. (In those days vacuum flasks were not cheap like today).

With that I decided to return to the site and bring my bag and flask back home

Because I didn't have my own transport it meant catching a bus from Lower Higham which was about a mile and a half away from our house.

But then I noticed my brother Alan's motorcycle parked outside the front gate.

And so, without any thought of the consequences, I callously *jump-started* his lovely motorcycle and off I went.

It was dark by now and I put on the headlights.

As I approached the Cliffe village I came to a curve in the road.

I was going too fast and lost control.

The next thing I knew was being wheeled into **Gravesend General Hospital** on a trolley with nurses and others around me.

I was x-rayed and given injections and treatment for my injuries, which included several stitches in and around my mouth, a cut over the eye, three cracked ribs, few scratches on my face and a sprained wrist.

Some of my bottom teeth were loosened in the accident and the doctor was going to remove them. But I would have none of that and despite them wanting to keep me in hospital I discharged myself.

It was about 10:30 in the evening and all I could think of was getting a drink before closing time at 11.00. And so, the first thing I did when I got out of there was to go to **The Railway Tavern**, - my favourite pub in Gravesend.

I remember a couple of girls who I knew quite well, shying away from me when I walked through the door. In fact, I heard someone scream when I pushed my way through the crowd to the bar.

I couldn't blame them as I must have looked a bit like **"Frankenstein's Monster."**

I had one arm in a sling, a bandaged head and stiches in my face.

My right eye was closed and bruised, and my clothes were damaged and torn and covered in my blood.

And despite all this, all I wanted was another drink.

Not once at that point, did I think about my poor brother who would be devastated that his lovely pride and joy **Triumph Bonneville** motorcycle was now wrecked and laying in an orchard on the outskirts of Cliffe village.

Not once did I think of my mum or dad or the rest of my family about how this would all affect their Christmas.

No. All I could think of was **me, me, me**.

I still cannot remember getting home afterwards and what it was like.

I believe my brain has a mechanism for shutting out some of my most *shameful memories.*

What I learned later was that despite all this, I'd had a lucky escape from perhaps a far more serious condition.

As it happened, just a second or two before crashing through the fence and into the orchard, I saw the headlights of a car in the distance. This road had very little traffic under normal conditions and sometimes there would be no activity at all for periods 10 or 15 minutes at a time, especially on a holiday period like now.

Miraculously, the occupants of the car were in fact my best friend *Nobby,* who was driving, and his girlfriend - (and future wife), *Jackie.*

He told me later that when they reached the site of the accident, I was jerking around in the road **"like an injured rabbit"** were the words he used.

I was covered in blood, and they both managed to get me into his car and took me straight to the hospital in Gravesend. (To this day I have absolutely no recollection of this - probably because I was concussed at the time.).

Over the years, I have had several *"moments"* that could have been life threatening. But something has always been there to get me through.

Today I believe that *"something"* to be God. I will just leave it there for now as my god cannot be adequately described.

Marriage & divorce

One day I met a girl I simply couldn't get out of my head—the woman who would eventually become my wife.

The twist was that she was someone my brother Alan had been seeing before I came on the scene.

I first saw her when she called for him at Mum's place. I was home on leave from the sea, and the moment I set eyes on her I was hooked. It took about three years after that before I finally asked Maggie out properly, but once I did, that was that.

At the time, some people would have described my drinking as "heavy." To me, it was normal. That about sums it up.

Looking back—honestly—I can say I managed to convince Maggie that my drinking was under control, and that marriage would change everything. It did, to some extent... but I still drank too much. By then I was working ashore as a labourer—hod carrier, scaffolder—whatever paid best on the building sites.

We decided to marry, and I asked Maggie to arrange for me to speak to her father. It was set for the following Sunday afternoon.

It was obvious her mum and dad didn't really approve of me, but I was determined. Maggie and I had already chosen the date: 19th June 1965, the day after her 18th birthday.

So, Mervyn—her dad—and I went into the living room. I was nervous because I knew he didn't think much of me, but I went straight to the point.

I said something like, "Mr H., I'm going to marry Margaret, and I'd like your approval—for her sake."

He looked at me and we sat there for a moment, just staring at each other. Then he said, "I don't suppose it will make any difference to you if I refuse."

I replied, "No, it wouldn't. We're determined to get married. But it would mean a lot to her if you gave your blessing."

Then he asked, "What are your ambitions for the future?"

"Just to make her happy," I said.

I think he was expecting something about a career, not the answer I gave. Still, he stood up, held out his hand, and we shook hands. In time I came to like and respect Mervyn a great deal.

His wife, Eva, was another matter. She always smiled and was *"nicey-nicey"* with me, but I could sense the dislike underneath. Having said that, they were both outwardly helpful to us in the early years and they made it possible for us to buy our house in Gordon Road, Strood. They provided basic furniture, and Mervyn acted as guarantor for the building society that gave us the mortgage.

The house was a three-bedroom terrace built around 1919, with a small front garden and a back garden about twelve metres long. You entered a passage with the staircase ahead, the living room on the left, then further down the passage another door on the left into the back room. Through that was the kitchen, and right at the back was the bathroom.

Once we moved in, Maggie and I decided the house would suit us better if we opened it up by combining the living room with back room. That meant knocking through the dividing wall and inserting a lintel to support the joists above.

I investigated the space under the floorboards and decided there was enough room to bury the rubble. I checked with a local timber merchant for a suitable hardwood lintel. I estimated the main work would take two full days, so I planned it for a weekend.

At about four o'clock on Saturday morning I moved the furniture and covered it with protective sheets. I stripped the wallpaper and plaster from both sides of the wall, then punched two holes through and inserted two needles—timber sections about 100mm by 100mm. I placed Acrow props under each needle, two on either side, and tightened them to take the load.

Then I started demolition.

By late morning the wall was down, and I went to collect the lintel. It was about nine feet long, four inches thick, eight inches deep—hardwood—and must have weighed forty-five kilos. The man at the timber yard asked where my truck was. I pointed to my right shoulder.

He helped balance that lintel onto me, and I carried it the mile from Rochester Bridge to Gordon Road. Even though I was very fit in those days, it was a brutal walk—mostly uphill.

Back home, I rested for a few minutes and got on with it. I had to open up the pockets for the lintel to sit in, and that was a struggle on my own, but I managed. Once the lintel was in, I could remove the props and needles, then mark and trim the opening.

Using hammer and chisel, I scored the wall carefully from top to bottom before continuing, keeping the dust down by spraying water as I worked. I lifted a few floorboards so I could drop bricks and mortar into the void and push the rubble further under the living room.

By about 9:30 p.m. the opening was complete—roughly two metres wide, almost full height, with the lintel above. I was exhausted, but I was pleased with myself. The plan was simple: shower, a few beers, sleep. Sunday would be another long day.

Early Sunday morning I framed out the opening and fixed it in place. Then I mixed plaster and covered the exposed brickwork and lintel, both sides. By late afternoon it had dried enough for the first coat of seraphite, followed by the second coat. After that it was just paint and paper.

I'd already bought the paint and wallpaper, and within a few more hours the job was done.

Because we knew the house would look like a bomb site while I worked, Maggie stayed at her parents over the weekend. On Sunday evening I rang to tell her it was finished. When she came round with her dad, he could hardly believe I'd done it alone. He assumed I'd had help.

Even the next-door neighbour, Peter—a jobbing builder—told me that if he'd taken it on, he'd have needed four or five days to do what I'd done in two. I was proud of it then, and that's why I mention it. I was driven by determination and had the energy to match. Today I couldn't do it in two weeks, even if I was foolish enough to try.

I was fit, I worked hard, and I was always chasing what we called "the big shilling."

Around this time, I became a subcontractor. I had a job in Sittingbourne for Parhams the builders. I employed four bricklayers and one hod-carrier, and each week I collected the cheque, cashed it, and on Saturday lunchtime we all went to the pub where I handed out the money.

I had even enrolled at Medway College of Technology for a Quantity Surveying course—one full day a week plus several evenings.

Here's the problem: I split the take equally between us—including myself— while also taking a day off each week for college. In other words, I lost out every week and didn't have the sense to see it. No other subcontractor did it that way. I just wasn't cut out for business, I suppose.

We were paying a mortgage and in 1967 our daughter was born. We named her Karen Margaret. And then—within eighteen months—Maggie and I separated.

We divorced sometime later. The divorce was granted to me on the grounds of Maggie's adultery, but that doesn't mean I was blameless. I could have been a better husband, and I could certainly have been a more responsible father. That's the truth of it.

The divorce devastated me. I went on a spree of drinking and reckless behaviour. I was heartbroken and, looking back, I think I went to pieces.

I'd always liked a drink and often had too much—but now my drinking changed into something else entirely. I became unreliable and lost job after job. We sold the house in Gordon Road cheaply and split the meagre proceeds.

After the legal formalities were done, I went to work in Jersey. The pattern there was simple: work a few days, earn decent money, then stop and go on the booze. Work again, stop again. Repeatedly. I had no ambitions. I was trying to get myself together, but I had no direction.

I still loved Margaret, despite everything, but although she asked—before we sold the house—whether we could try again, I knew there could be no reconciliation. Not ever. That chapter was closed.

I missed Karen terribly. But at a meeting with a children's welfare officer—before Margaret and her new man, Ernie T. were to marry—I was advised it would be best for Karen if I stayed away, so she could have a *"normal"* upbringing with her mother and stepfather.

When I told Mum what had been said, she and my sister were deeply upset. They tried to convince me not to accept it. But I believed the welfare people knew best. They dealt with cases like ours all the time, and I assumed their advice came from experience.

The truth is, I was confused and miserable and overwhelmed. I wanted to run— run from everything. That is the sad truth, however wrong and spineless it may sound now. I didn't have the courage or strength to do anything else at the time.

Mum told me I would regret it later. She was right. I have regretted it all my life, but there's no changing what's already done

Jersey

I wanted to run and that's what I did. I had been to Jersey in the Channel Islands a couple or so years previously and though it would be a good idea to go there again and start afresh. I just wanted to be away from Kent and all the memories. I was so miserable.

I had a few pounds, not very much at all, and got a flight to Jersey. I booked into a cheap B&B after getting the airport bus into St. Helier.

Within a couple of days, I met two fellows in a pub who were building a perimeter wall around a private house on the outskirts of the town. This led to us three working on the wall. We would start around daylight each morning, work like maniacs for about 5 or 6 hours and that would be it. We had earned enough, so it was pub time. And that's how it was.

When one job fished we'd start another soon after. Pete was from Sydney Australia and Hector was from Dublin in Eire. We all got on well, at work and in the pub.

Although I was earning well from this casual work I was spending well too, although I surprised myself because I actually saved a bit too.

Italy: Ostia

For a while I went to Italy, to a place outside Rome called Lido di Ostia. At first I stayed with a British couple who were travelling with a small caravan. They let me sleep in their provisions tent.

When they moved on, I ended up living on the beach with a group of Romanian gypsies. We bought coconuts in the market, sliced them up, and sold them to holidaymakers on the beach.

This was during the Vietnam War, when America was losing, and many young American men of conscription age fled to Europe to avoid being drafted. I became friendly with several of them. One of them, Paul, is worth mentioning.

Paul's father was a serving Colonel in the United States Army. He had advance knowledge that conscription was coming, and Paul persuaded him to allow him to "study" at a college in Rome. We used to party on the beach with other dodgers too, including some Australians avoiding conscription in their own country.

Compared to most of us, Paul was wealthy—he owned an 8mm movie camera. We had endless fun making silly films on the beach, dressing up and acting out scenes. Paul was director, producer, scriptwriter, cameraman... everything. We had to do it his way, but it was great fun.

While I was there I met a German girl named Anna. She was travelling after graduating from university in Cologne and could speak five or six languages. She was incredibly clever. I often wonder whether she ever finished her world tour. Her next stop was Sicily, and once she left Ostia we lost touch.

Back to Jersey

I can't remember exactly when—or why—I left Italy, but after a time I ended up back in Jersey.

There I fell in with a fellow called John McC. We called him "Cash", for reasons I can't explain, because he was always broke. Cash was the son of a successful builder from Leigh in Lancashire, and he was married to a lovely girl he'd left back home while he gallivanted around Jersey, playing the field with holidaymakers.

I didn't like the way he treated his wife, but he was good company and we had plenty of laughs.

Another mate was Peter, a bricklayer from Middlesbrough—also good fun, and a proper character.

I found lodging with a family in a huge house. The mother—Nan—was a Jersey girl, and her husband—Davy—was from Glasgow. I had a large room to myself with an en-suite bathroom, which felt like luxury.

Davy was a decent man, and unusual for a Glaswegian in one respect: he didn't drink alcohol.

Then something happened that changed everything.

A close friend of Davy's was given a serious hiding by people who had travelled to Jersey specifically to mete out that punishment. His friend ended up in hospital. Davy was furious, and what followed was a chain of events that ruined him.

First, Davy went searching through the pubs for the culprits. He picked up a drink—and got drunk.

Then he went home, concealed a sawn-off shotgun inside his overcoat, and went out looking for them.

He believed they would be at a bookmaker's shop opposite the hospital and waited there.

Then he fired the shotgun at the bookmaker's premises, smashing the windows.

He was quickly overpowered and arrested.

A few days later he was in court and sentenced to two years in prison, which devastated Nan and the children.

I'll never know for certain, but I often wondered whether Davy was like me—someone who could take one drink and then be unable to stop. Perhaps that's why he avoided alcohol in the first place. Either way, one choice led to another, and his life was altered forever.

It wasn't long after that tragedy that I left Jersey for the mainland—and this is how it happened.

The Getaway

One morning Peter and Cash came to see me and told me what had happened the day before.

Cash had got into a fight with a man and knocked him down a flight of stairs in the apartment block where he was living. The man was in hospital, and the police were looking for Cash.

I should have stayed out of it, but they pleaded with me. They knew I had a Merchant Navy background and assumed I might be able to get them off the island on the ferry from St Helier to Weymouth without going through the usual security checks.

So, I contacted a man I knew on the ferries and made my decision. I told Cash and Peter to be ready to leave the following evening on the night sailing.

None of us had money for tickets, so I arranged for one of the crew to meet us on the dock and slip us aboard quietly. And it worked.

We sailed that night for Weymouth.

During the crossing, Peter somehow managed to get drunk—despite the fact the three of us were broke. In his drunken state he opened the pens where passengers' pet dogs were kept on the upper deck.

It was hilarious watching crew members chasing dogs all over the place trying to get them back into the pens. Then it wasn't hilarious anymore.

One of the dogs fell over the side and was lost at sea.

Trains Without Tickets

When we reached Weymouth we sneaked onto the London train. We managed to avoid the ticket inspector and got off at Paddington.

Then we pulled the same trick again, travelling from Euston up to Manchester. Somehow we arrived without being caught. We waited there for a mate of Cash to meet us with a van, and then drove on to Leigh, where Cash came from.

Leigh

Cash managed to borrow some money from either his mother or his father—I'm not sure which—and we headed straight to the pub.

It was there that I met Alan H. (known as Ali). His parents had died, leaving him the tenancy of a council house. Ali was broke as usual, but when I said I needed somewhere to doss for a while, he didn't hesitate. He offered me a roof over my head.

The house had barely any furniture. What little there had been, he'd either sold—or broken up and burned for firewood. I slept on the kitchen floor, on cold lino over concrete. It was absolutely freezing.

After a few days I got work on the new town project at Runcorn in Cheshire. The first thing I did was get a sub on my wages and buy a bag of coal so we could have some heat in that ice-cold house.

Ali was good-natured, but looking back, he was chronically alcoholic. He had literally burned his own furniture to keep warm. There were no beds. Not even a table. Everything had gone into the fire.

He stole lead off the roofs of buildings and had been caught several times. The local police knew him well and sometimes just locked him up overnight, so he'd be warm in the cells.

A Brush with Fame

It was during this time I met Georgie F., who was a popular singer and pianist then and often appeared on television programmes like *Ready Steady Go*. He was a local lad from Leigh and surprisingly down-to-earth despite his success. He'd come into our pub whenever he was back visiting family. I got to know him slightly and liked him—just an ordinary bloke.

Leigh itself was typical of northern towns at that time. Everyone seemed to know everyone. There was always banter—good-humoured and constant. Even early in the morning, when people were rushing to catch buses for work, they'd shout across the street to each other and plan for the pub later. It felt very different from the south of England.

Work, Money, and London Again

After about three weeks on the Runcorn project, I picked up some subcontract work from another subcontractor. That allowed me to earn decent money and take on a few others—bricklayers, scaffolders, whoever was needed.

Eventually I heard of a well-paid project in the London area, so I came south again. This time I had two subcontracts—one in Lewisham, another in Orpington.

I spent plenty of time around Bayswater—clubs, pubs, the lot. I met one or two female companions, but nothing serious. I wasn't interested in getting involved again with anyone. Not ever. That's how I felt then.

I drifted back to sea for a few trips here and there.

Then I found out Mum was having health problems and returned to Kent to see her. That led to me living with Mum and Dad again for a while.

I worked wherever I could, and at night I went out—pubs, clubs, late finishes. I'd come home from work, eat a meal Mum had prepared, go to the pub, then on to a nightclub until the early hours, and get home around three in the morning. I'd sleep three hours, get up, and go and do another day's work wherever it happened to be.

I never gave a second thought to the fact that Mum—and Dad too—were worried sick about the way I was living.

They wanted me to settle down again. But I wouldn't hear of it.

Westminster Dredging

One day I met a man whose wife used to be a teacher at the primary school in Higham. He knew I had been going to sea previously and introduced me to a man who was the personnel manager for *Westminster Dredging Company.*

I was offered a job as a deckhand on a barge. The money was good, and I got some promotion after a while.

I worked for them for a while on different projects around the UK. I finally came to be working on a dredging project at Weymouth in Dorset. The dredger was a grab unit called the *"Tilbury Toiler"*

The job was progressing quite well until the local Agent for the company informed us, we were not entitled to have a cook.

We had a locally employed cook who came daily to the dredge and prepared our food.

The Agent told us we would have to use one of the existing crew to do this job.

He summarily fired the cook, paid him off, and went ashore leaving us to get on with our work.

Our senior *Dredge master* was a long-term employee named *Ken G.* The brother of Ken was also an employee of Westminster Dredging Company at head office in Gravesend.

Ken Gillet called all the crew together and we had a meeting onboard. The outcome was to stop the work until the cook was reinstated.

It took about half a day to disengage the operation and bring the dredger alongside one of the jetties in the river. When we were done, we sent for the Agent.

He arrived and pompously ordered us to get the operation going again. We refused to follow this instruction, and he was on and off the phone to the head office for several hours.

Eventually, he came back to us and had the local cook with him. The cook had been drinking all day long and was quite drunk but that didn't matter to us. We had won the day. Then we broke out the dredge and all other equipment, got back on station and continued with the project.

But our stoppage was not only costly to Westminster Dredging Company, but it was also unprecedented. This sort of thing would not, could not be allowed to be repeated either by our crew or any other in the fleet. *We had crossed a line*

The following day, a completely new crew arrived in Weymouth. The smug Agent was as pleased as punch when he summoned us all and told us to report to the office in Gravesend. We were finished on this project. These were the instructions from the Head Office.

I phoned the Gravesend office and was told to report on Monday morning to a motorised split barge named the *"Borough Deep"* which was operating on the river Thames.

I did so and halfway through the morning I was summoned by the master of the vessel. He told me there was a message from the Gravesend office for me to report there, with my kit, to the *Personnel Manager*.

Arriving at the HEAD office I was shown into his office. *The Personnel Manager - Mr. Paul A.,* was very courteous and asked me what had happened at Weymouth. I told him the truth without making any excuse for my part.

He fired me there and then.

And that was the end of my experience with the company. I was blacklisted with Westminster Dredging company.

The Senior Dredge-master (Ken G.) was reprimanded and downgraded in position. Two other long-term employees were suspended from duty for two months.

And the rest? Well, like me, they were all sacked.

But life goes on, vacancies are there if you look for them and shortly after I was offered a job in dredging at Felixstowe where a new dock was to be built.

This was late 1971. I started as deckhand (again) and after a few weeks I was promoted.

Again, after a few more weeks, I was put on permanent night shift in charge of a new C.S.D. (Cutter Suction Dredger). We worked 12 hours on and 12 hours off 7 days a week. I was back-to-back with the senior dredge-master – *Nick C.*, a fellow with a lot of dredging experience

This job was very well paid, and we would work 3 weeks on and one (long) weekend off. It suited me fine.

In November '72, there was a very bad storm. I came on duty early morning as it was my turn on dayshift for that week. This was just when the weather started to get bad.

The dredging superintendent *Rudd D.* called me on the v.h.f. to batten the dredger down and leave it on storm anchors and bring everyone ashore. This was happening all over the project with other offshore equipment. This storm was predicted to be a bad one.

I told him that if we left it to the mercy of the storm it might sink. He insisted that I followed his instructions.

As I was now the master of this (small) dredger I decided unilaterally that I was not going to abandon the vessel. I thought that if some of us stayed on-board there was little chance of the vessel floundering.

Together we got cracking to do the needful, lashing everything down and battening hatches and doors etc. We had a tugboat standing by on the lee side ready to take us ashore.

Again, the call from the superintendent came for me to get everyone onshore right away.

But I asked first for three volunteers to stay on-board with me, and we would ride out the impending storm. Only one man would stay, and he was the newest and least experienced man.

In my heart, I was very critical of the more experienced crewmembers. Some of them had been much longer in this dredging industry than I had but I had to allow them to go ashore if it was their choice. And they had the backing of the Marine Superintendent.

And so, the crew went ashore leaving me and the new-recruit on-board the vessel.

As the storm built up in intensity it was apparent it was going to be a bad one. (And it was – the worst storm on the East coast since 1953).

During the night as the seas got bigger and the wind got stronger, I could hear distress calls going out on the v.h.f. from vessels in the area.

"May-Day May-Day" was all we could hear and to be honest I was quite scared. I thought at that time that I had made another very bad decision, and we both should have left with the others.

But it was too late now. There was not a single vessel that could now approach to rescue us. It was far too late for that to happen as the sea state was horrendous by now.

But I could not expose my fear to this new guy, or he might panic. Apart from that, I knew that if I did not focus on one thing only (staying afloat) we would not see tomorrow - either of us. And the poor fellow was obviously already regretting that he had volunteered to stay with me.

I had to try to make out that all was well on our vessel that our anchors were good that our vessel was new, was properly secured, and was watertight. We would get through this I kept telling him.

We worked like dogs for most of that awful night using our winches to always try to keep our head into the direction of the seas. But sometime during the night he came onto the bridge as white as a ghost. He was in panic.

I said what's the matter with you. It will be ok. Don't worry.

He told me that one of the glass sight panels on the engine room bulkhead had been caved in. These panels were about 1 metre long by about 30 cm high and were situated in the bulkhead of the engine room to provide light. (The same function as a skylight only on a vertical bulkhead).

The glass was about 40mm thick and normally any sea hitting it would not damage it. They were supposed to be storm proof, so I assumed it must have been hit by a heavy piece of flotsam that was all over the sea by now. Looking back, it could have been a fault with the sealing.

Anyway, I told him to stay on the bridge and man the radio and the winches whilst I had a look below. When I reached a safe zone to assess the damage, I could see water pouring into the engine room each time a wave surged over the main deck.

Already I could see the water had reached the engine room deck plates meaning the bilges were already filling up.

Under normal circumstances if water reaches a certain level the bilge pumps would kick in automatically. And of course, they had done so.

But in this case, the bilge pumps were incapable of handling the volume. I had to do something I had never tried before. I went into the pump room and disconnected a pipe on the suction side of the dredge pump itself.

I arranged a flexible suction hose about 30cm in diameter to be submerged in the rising waters. This must have taken about half an hour and the water in the pump room was around my knees by the time I'd finished. I made my way back to the bridge and started the Main Engine.

I then engaged the dredge pump coupling and watched the instruments to see if I would get enough suction pressure.

Nothing happened, and the fear hit me. It would not prime like this. If the pump could not prime it could note create pressure (i.e. suction). I rushed back down to the Engine room and saw the water had now reached the lower part of the auxiliary engine.

If the water got into the oil sump it was all over. The engine would stop and immediately after that, the main engine would stop.

The vessel would sink, and I knew we would never be able to survive in those seas. To be honest I though *"this is it, this is my last day"*.

I then heard a noise from the pump room and rushed through the compartment. There I could see the flexible suction hose threshing around in the sump and I knew the pump had now primed itself and had begun to remove the water from the bilges.

I worked my way back onto the bridge. The man there was as white as a ghost. I went over to him and said something. I can't remember what it was I said to him but whatever it was it seemed to calm him.......

Now dawn was breaking, and this made a huge difference. Although the seas were still raging at least we could get a better perspective. When it's dark in those conditions it can be quite scary because everything to be hugely exaggerated.

Now we could see things that we hadn't been able to see during the darkness of the night. There were small boats and sailing vessels just thrown up on the shoreline as if they were toys.

We could see our floating pipeline that transported our dredging spoil from dredger to reclaim area just smashed up and sections of it lodged and trapped underneath the jetty to the West of us. This was over 800 linear metres of 550mm diameter steel pipes with a 15mm wall thickness just twisted and torn apart like plastic.

This was a **methane jetty** and if those methane pipes had been ruptured the whole place could have exploded. But it didn't. We were so lucky.

There were several other things that happened. We had to face another night of terror before the seas subsided enough for a tugboat to eventually come to us and put a relief crew on board our vessel. This was around mid-day.

It had been over 40 hours since we two came on-board and we were quite exhausted. Today I could not take 20% of what we had to endure – it would kill me.

Everyone made a fuss of me, but I insisted the real hero was the new fellow. If he had not stayed, then perhaps we might have sunk. I remember thinking at the time how this young fellow, *the brand-new recruit,* stayed with me when all the others did the sensible thing and went ashore. If something happened and he was lost in this horrible storm and I somehow survived, how would I ever explain to his parents that it was because of me that he was lost. Perhaps this inspired my courage instead of being overwhelmed by fear. I have often since thought about it. I could never have managed alone what needed to be done over those hours. But it's something we shall never know.

I do know one thing. That fellow NEVER came back to our vessel. In fact, he didn't even come back to the office to collect the money he was due. I guess he made up his mind that it was not the kind of work he was looking for, eh? The worst thing of all is that despite all my years of journaling I can find no record of his name.

In fact, a survey vessel and two other dredgers on the same project did sink because of the storm and it was later concluded that had a crew been onboard they may have been prevented from sinking.

The company made a fuss of me, and I received a quite generous ex-gratia payment. I got my picture in the papers etc. and they blew the story out of proportion. It didn't do me any harm though. *Or did it?*

Self-esteem is good in a balanced measure, but it can also lead to unwarranted self-importance if the balance is out of kilter. Perhaps it *did do me harm* in a way I only saw much later in my life.

Now I was being feted by people I'd never previously set eyes on, and it must have gone to my head. There was always a pint waiting for me in the bars I frequented in Felixstowe, left by somebody or another. I was treated - (for a short period only I must add), like a celebrity.

CHAPTER 5 June

The love of my life.

I was living in a nice 6 berth caravan on the Felixstowe Park which was a short walk to the docks. I would walk to work (10mins) and get the boat out to where my dredger was operating.

One evening during the summer I got back to my caravan and went off for a shower in the shower block nearby.

When I got back, I noticed an attractive blonde woman outside a rental holiday caravan close to my own caravan. She asked me if I could help as she'd locked herself out. Anyway, this led to me speaking to her friend *June* and I was immediately attracted to her.

And so, after chatting with her on and off over the next 24 hours, I asked her if she'd let me take her out for a meal, and she agreed. We got on well from the start and I took her out several times in the week she was on holiday,

By the time she was leaving, we had arranged to meet up again in London. We met at Trafalgar Square and had a lovely time together.

This led to us agreeing to set up home together and I rented a lovely apartment at the area called *Undercliff.*

It had beautiful views over the beaches and out to sea. It was perfect. I knew June would love it. She was expected to bring her stuff in a couple of weeks, and we had plans to make a life together.

All seemed well. But we all know what *Rabbie Burns* said about the best laid plans of mice and men......

I found I was drinking increasingly and even taking booze to work. One night, when I was working offshore on the dredger, I decided to go to the pub because I needed a drink and there was none onboard.

I just stopped the whole operation and took a boat ashore. My plan was to come back later and start up again.

I knew my productivity rate was the high and I would make up for the hour or so I intended to be onshore. I did come back and started up again as if nothing I had done was wrong. I have since learned that a drunken idea is not amongst our best, most reliable or sensible ideas. The very next morning I was sacked. This was totally justified, and I knew it.

Question: What did I learn from this lesson?

Answer: Don't get too big for your boots. No-one and I mean *no-one* is indispensable.

A costly lesson for me but one that I would stupidly repeat several times more in my career before it really sunk into my thick skull.

When June arrived with her ten-year old son Chris came to Felixstowe and our lovely apartment, they were both very happy with the apartment and to see me.. Then I dropped the bombshell about losing my job. She didn't think it was too important. She just said she would get a job, and we would get by until I was able to get placed again.

She did get a job in a hairdresser salon and later in a café called *"Nuts and Honey"*. My mum and dad paid us a visit during this time during a very cold period with ice everywhere.

A few days after she arrived, I was in the pub (as usual) and met *Alan R.* who was the **Dredging Superintendent** in another company on the project. He heard I was looking for work and offered to arrange an interview for me with a guy called *Mike S.*

At that time, Mike S. was UK manager for a Dutch dredging company called **Cunis-Delta-Bouw.** They traded under the name of Land Salvage in UK.

Anyway, I travelled down to Essex by train to meet Mike S. in his office.

He asked me why I left my previous job, and I told him I got the sack and the reason why. He asked me if I had a drinking problem. *Who…? me?*

I promptly denied it and told him that it was a one-off mistake, and I promised him it would never happen again.

He said he *"knew all about"* it and I wanted to see if I was honest. *"You have a job if you want it"* he said. I asked what the job was.

He told me there was a channel being dredged in the North of Scotland for an oil rig facility and it was behind schedule.

He wanted me to try to get it back on target as it was costing the company money.

I asked what kind of authority I would be granted to achieve the target.

He told me that I would have full authority over all offshore activities and would report only to the Project Manager, a *Mr. Frank B.*

I would have a free hand in most things. The important thing was to get the team motivated, plan the operations in such a way as to increase our productivity, turn the job around sufficiently to make profitable.

This prospect excited me, and I was flattered that he had this much faith in my abilities. I was determined not to let him down.

He also warned me to watch my drinking. *"You are going to mix with a few heavy drinkers up there"* he said. With that he sent me to the secretary who provided a plane ticket voucher and some petty cash for expenses etc.

I signed a contract of employment which I hardly read through in detail as I was so keen to take the job and did not want to find any *"small print"* that would deter me.

Scotland

Getting off the plane (A Dan Air Dakota DC8) at Dalcross Airport in Ardersier, I was met by a driver for the company called *"Fergie"*.

He took me to a small town about 4 miles away called Nairn.

I checked into the Royal Hotel, - (a real dive), and he told me he would come for me in the morning to take me to meet *Frank B*.

Mindful that I needed to be careful about how much I drank I just had a pint in the hotel bar before going out to explore the town. What a dump it was. It was so depressing.

The people seemed to be talking a foreign language. The buildings were drab. And the worst thing of all (for me at least) was the shock of finding out that pubs in Scotland closed at 9:00pm.

How I would be able to survive in this *"back of beyond"* place I could not imagine. The next morning Fergie showed up and took me to the site in the company vehicle.

Here I met Angus (Angie) who was employed to look after the canteen on the site. He made the best bacon rolls I had ever tasted and was a nice chap. Everyone liked Angie.

Frank B. came in around 9:00 am and I was introduced to him. He then introduced me to his sidekick, Bob G. I liked Bob right away but I he was a bit wary of me at first. Frank explained that they had two small dredgers working on the project.

The scope of work was dredging an access channel for barges to come alongside a wharf that was under construction. It was a very straightforward project, and the substrata was lightly dense sand.

The main problem the company was facing was low productivity of the dredging operations. The resulting delays were leading to liquidated damages being threatened by the main contractor.

Now Frank stressed to me that my job was to intervene in the operations in the role of dredging supervisor and solve the problems being faced. I was ok with that and told him to make clear to all the employees what my role was and to stress to them all that I needed their full cooperation.

I had been around long enough to know that there were bound to be some people already in the company that would resent a newcomer being in authority over them. I told Frank very clearly that if I encountered any resistance at all to my proposals, I would send them ashore, and they would not be coming back. I expected him to back me on this when it happens.

He was ok with that, and I then began moving onto the floating and shore-based units to meet the crews and others in the workforce.

One of the first things I discovered was that there were enormous amounts of kelp on the seabed. This kelp had the effect of clogging up the suction mouths of each dredger and these obstructions had a direct effect on the rate of productivity.

And so, we introduced a clearing operation of the seabed to minimise the quantity of kelp when we dredged. To do this we hired a piece of equipment from a local farmer which acted as a rake. We prepared a towing bridle for the rake, and it was towed by one of our workboats over the pre-dredged area. This operation continued until enough kelp had been removed to allow clearer access to the seabed itself. Only then were the cutter suction dredgers deployed in the previously cleared area.

After a few weeks we were making significant increases to our productivity and progress on the job gained momentum. Increased productivity was being achieved, and I now began to feel comfortable in my position.

I had taken on several new employees and although none had previous experience in dredging works, they were very adaptable and did what was asked of them and more.

Two of these new guys were brothers and they were quite notorious in the area for their drinking and fighting. These were Jockie and Donald W.

These two young fellows would argue with the stones in the road and fight *anyone* at the drop of a hat, but they were fearless of the sea.

And on this project, that was an asset as we often faced bad weather conditions.

However, they would do everything I asked of them and never once did they give me any trouble - (personally). I was proud to have them on the team.

We often encountered bad weather conditions in the *Moray Firth,* and I could always rely on these two if I needed volunteers for some dangerous or unusually risky work. They would always be there with me where other more experienced men would back off citing that it was too risky.

I won't go into details but some of the work was very risky. However, that is the nature of dredging in hostile waters, it's just a part of the job.

I was traveling up and down to Felixstowe every two or three weeks to see my June. We had set up our home in the apartment at *Undercliff Apartments.*

It was a lovely place, and we enjoyed being there, but when I had to fly back to Scotland after 4 days at home it was awful - for both of us. One day I came home, and June had packed all her stuff. She made it clear that she was coming back with me to Scotland. Her ex-husband had obtained a court-order preventing us from taking Chris to Scotland on the grounds that the difference in Scottish and English legal systems would not be compatible with the previously issued custody order. So, for the time being, Chris was to stay with his father.

And so, June and I vacated the apartment and packed all our worldly belongings into 3 suitcases. It was almost Christmas and the company had agreed that the English personnel would have the Christmas period off, and the Scots personnel would have the New Year (Hogmanay) period off. The project would just have mainly maintenance coverage in these two holiday breaks.

In view of this, June and I were going to say with June's mum and dad in Redbourn over Christmas.

And so, we caught a train with all our possessions in our 3 suitcases and some bags to Ipswich then piled onto a Greenline bus from Ipswich to Redbourn.

June's brother-in-law *Bryan* took some of the stuff in his car and we sent this as freight to Inverness railway depot by train to be collected later.

We had a lovely family Christmas and on or around 28th December we took the Dan Air flight from Heathrow to Dalcross airport.

We arrived at Inverness airport on a very cold evening with snow on the ground.

June was as white as a ghost, and I could hardly see her against the backdrop of the snow. She blended in perfectly.........hahaha.

We checked in at the lodging house which we nicknamed *"Kinky Cottage"*. We were taken there by my pal *Mike H*.

Mike was part of the English crowd who were on the project and who travelled up from England and also stayed at *"Kinky Cottage"* whilst in Scotland.

The landlady was an English person, and she was as tight as the proverbial *"ducks' arse"*.

There was never enough hot water, and we often had to bathe on tepid water after a long hard day's work.

No matter how much we all complained about it, things never improved. The food was poor quality and never enough on the plate. *Even the cat turned its nose up at some of the fish she served us.*

After several days of this I knew that changes had to be made. It was quite an awful place to live. And so, after much searching, I managed to find a caravan that I could rent. It cost about 7 pounds a week, was quite tiny, but it made such a difference. We were very happy in that tiny little caravan. It had a bathroom and the bath itself was about the size of old-fashioned kitchen sink. But at least the water was HOT.

One day I came home from work and June was beaming all over her face. She told me she was pregnant. We were over the moon about this and promptly went off to celebrate.

After living in the caravan for several months we were lucky enough to be allocated a council house in the village of Ardersier. This happened for two reasons.

1. I was considered a Key Worker in the new oil industry.

2. June was carrying a child in her womb, and the caravan was damp and deemed to be unsuitable under these new circumstances.

It was wonderful news. The house we had been offered was in Station Road, Ardersier. It had two bedrooms, a garden back and front and a full-sized bath in the separate bathroom. **Absolute PARADISE to us.**

We spent some cash and over a period we furnished it nicely and to our liking. It was lovely. The main entertainment sources in the village were the 4 village pubs.

My favourite was the *Alma* owned by *Ian and Margaret A.* They were such a fun couple, and we had many great evenings in that place.

In those days the pubs closed at 9:00pm and we would rush home from work and straight into the pub after a clean-up and a quick bite to eat prepared by June.

Sometimes I would get home after the pub closed and then have my supper. It was hard on June, but she took it all on-board.

Our son was born in May 1975, and we gave him the name *Scott* after the son one of our dear friends.

As it happened, we did turn the job around, and I was given a nice bonus from *Mike S.*

It was in an envelope and equivalent to 2 months wages. In those days we were paid by the hour, and I was working a minimum 84 hours a week –sometimes 96 hours.

Eventually the project completed and the client - McDermott Company (USA), bought the dredgers and the marine craft from Land Salvage.

I was one of these taken on by McDermott and my pay jumped again. Now I was earning a good wage for those days. I was still drinking heavily but it seemed –*(to me),* that it was under control.

One day however a friend who was a marine engineer working with me offshore decided to move to Malta in the Mediterranean. This called for some kind of celebration and a bottle of whisky magically appeared from nowhere.

We were at work and of course alcohol was totally forbidden on site under company rules.

Rules had never been a strong deterrent to me up to now and of course with my attitude as it was in those days, it required minimal encouragement for me to take a drink or two.

What I would never acknowledge in those days was that when I took a drink the drink took me. One bottle became two and several of us then had a few nips apiece.

Someone mentioned to my boss that I was tippling, and I was called to his office.

My boss was a very decent guy. His name was **Harry T.** and I had a lot of respect for him.

He asked me point blank, *"Dougie, I was told you've been drinking on the job, but I don't believe it, but I have to ask you anyway"*.

The way he spoke and acted indicated that he was sending me a clear message to me *to deny that I had been drinking.*

But, instead of that I said *"Well yes Harry, I've had a few nips at site because one of my mates is leaving. Sorry for letting you down."*

He raised his eyebrows in disbelief that I had admitted this to him in front of two witnesses. But although I had understood his guarded message to me, I could not lie to him. I like the fellow and just couldn't lie to him.

Obviously, he had no alternative but to send me to the site doctor right away for assessment.

The doctor was my own GP in the village who was an excellent man and a very good doctor.

He breathalysed me and took a blood sample which showed a very high level of alcohol in my blood, (recorded as 255mg per ml.) - something like 3 times the legal limit permitted for driving a vehicle on the road in those days. Today the benchmark is 35mg, much lower than it was then.

I was tested for alcohol and found positive - well over the top. I was immediately suspended from duty. After an inquiry myself and another man who had also been caught drinking on the job, were found guilty of gross misconduct and sacked.

I was offered another job with a subcontractor in Kent, but by now June had joined me, we were married, had a son and a house so we were settled.

The locals had agreed to *"adopt us Sassenachs"* according to Fergie and we were having a nice life. Why fix something that was working we thought.

I was a bit remorseful for a day or two, but my policy was always, **when you get knocked down, get up and fight back.**

I knew that I would be able to find another job if I put myself about and just put losing the last job down to experience. I would never blame anyone but myself, which, on looking back, was one thing in my favour.

Scott II

Because I'd been fired from my last job, I was not entitled to any state benefits, and I quickly found myself a job as *Bargemaster* with *The British Waterways Board.*

My place of work was at the depot at Muirtown Lochs at the Eastern section of the Caledonian Canal.

The job was poorly paid and boring, and it - *(barely),* paid the rent. But I told June it would do for a short while until I could find something better.

One day the Canal Superintendent -John B., approached me and asked me if I could take over temporarily as skipper of the *Scott II.* This was a small passenger vessel that plied the Caledonian Canal and Loch Ness during the tourist season taking tourists on short cruises of about four hours.

I agreed, and because this was *slightly* better paid and a bit less boring.

One of the perks was that we had a bar onboard, and although my contract prohibited me - (as skipper), from drinking on duty, I could hardly refuse a dram or two from gracious tourists, could I? That would have been bad PR on my part would it not?

This small vessel was also classed as a registered ice breaker, as sometimes the freshwater canal freezes over in the winter, and this little old lady allowed vessels to move freely in those conditions.

I had a Polish engineer who had been employed on this vessel for 35 years or more. He was a *pain in the arse* sometimes, especially when he went on about having seen the Loch Ness Monster *(Nessie),* not once, but on several occasions.

One day, Mr. B. asked me to go to Lock Darroch and tow back the gate lifting barge that was moored up there for a job in Muirtown Locks.

I took the Scott II down to Lock Darroch and moored behind the gate lifter barge. I checked the water depth and each of the vessel's dimensions and decided to turn the barge in the canal at this point.

I instructed the crew on the procedure to follow, and the engineer came rushing onto the bridge demanding to know what I was doing.

I explained the plan to him, and he almost went ballistic saying it had never been done this way before and all the other skippers previously had towed the barge through the locks and into the Loch Ness. Then they turned it around and towed the barge back through the locks and then into the canal.

I explained that this would add 4-5 hours to a simple job of work, and we were going to do it the way I had planned.

He began to protest, and I had no choice but to order him off the bridge.

The operation went exactly to plan, and we were back at Muirtown with the barge by late afternoon.

The Superintendent Mr. B.was very surprised when we came alongside at Muirtown as he was not expecting us to arrive until late in the evening or the early hours of the next morning.

He asked me how I had managed to do it so quickly, but I just patted my nose to indicate it was my secret.

Sadly, this type of restrictive practice that the Polish engineer was trying to perpetuate was rife in UK workplaces in the 60's and 70's.

Is there is less of it today? Well, perhaps so. But with all the changes in the legislation about safe working practices, I think if I wanted to follow the same procedure as I write this sentence, it might not be allowed.

There's bound to be a rule that someone would point out that was being breached. But there I go again. I just can't help being a cynic can I?

But I think it true to say that many people have now woken up to the fact that restrictive practices are a primary cause that can lead to companies going bust, and that doesn't help anyone.

One very cold and wintry morning I was on the bridge of the Scott II doing a bit of paperwork when a man shouted to me from the jetty. I went out to see what he wanted, and he told me that something, a vehicle had gone into the canal.

I went along with him to where there were tyre marks leading from the slip road, over the grassed verge, down the slope and disappeared into the waters of the canal. The water as usual was dark and murky and I could see nothing below the surface. So, I ran back to the Muirtown Lock office and called the emergency services.

Then I called the yard British Waterways Yard at Clachnaharry where I knew our three divers could be found.

I spoke to the foreman, explained the situation, and requested that divers be sent with full kit to Muirtown Lock offices.

They arrived within 20 minutes or so and I showed them where the vehicle had entered the canal. By now we had the police presence, and the fire brigade also came.

Our divers went into the water and after a few minutes one of them surfaced indicating to me that there was a van down there and he could see a body inside.

Then he went down again and as he did so the other diver in the water surfaced and held up two fingers indicating two bodies.

Then the other one broke the surface once more holding up three fingers. Sadly, we really did have a disaster here. Three bodies inside a van had now to be recovered.

We arranged with the fire brigade to bring a mobile crane to the location. Our divers arranged the slings from a spreader beam and by late afternoon we had lifted the van out of the water.

The three bodies were removed and taken away. There were two women and one man. We learned later that the man was bringing an outboard engine from Fort William to the boat yard near to Muirtown Locks. His wife and her sister thought they would take the opportunity to come along with him and then they would do some shopping in Inverness before going back to Fort William. A sad ending to their plans for a day out. A sad day for those families.

Not too long after this, I found a better paid job. This time I became a scaffolder on a construction site in Inverness. The company was Holst Northwest.

I stayed with them for a while but as ever I was looking for better pay. It was always the bigger shilling I chased. Then I was put in touch with someone who was working on a new project in Kishorn.

Kishorn

Times were tough in the Highlands of Scotland in the '70's. Here's an example of why I say this.

I started working in Kishorn on the master platform that was under construction for the Ninian Oil field in the North Sea. I became one of those people who are still to this day referred to as *"The Kishorn Commandos".*

The original Kishorn Yard was developed as a manufacturing and fabrication yard for oil platforms in the 1970's.

The yard was owned by Howard Doris Ltd and operated until 1987.

In 1974, work began on the North side of Loch Kishorn to develop a substantial acreage to build the Ninian Central Platform.

This was by far the largest project undertaken at the site and the construction of the 150-metre diameter dry dock to house the first layer of the Ninian Central as it was 'set down' as a concrete structure.

At its peak point there were over 3,000 people working at the yard. Owing to planning and travel constraints the yard was to be considered as an island and all materials and people were to be brought in by sea or air.

Two retired cruise liners were moored in the Loch for workers accommodation; they were the *Rangatira* and the *Odysseus.*

As the *Ninian project* continued it was floated out into *Loch Kishorn,* at that time it weighed close to 150,000 tonnes.

The wet dock in Loch Kishorn has an almost unlimited depth for construction purposes at 80 metres. Upon completion the *600,000-tonne* concrete platform was towed by seven tugs to its North Sea location. At that time this was the largest man-made *moveable object* on the planet.

The client was **Chevron Oil,** and I was working for a sub-contractor- one of many at the site. The construction site, located on the NW coast of Scotland was near a place called Loch Carron.

From the day I arrived it rained. And I mean it rained stair-rods. And it rained for seven solid weeks. *Honestly, 7 weeks*.

The initial construction process for this massive structure took place in a hole that had been dug close to the Loch. The water of the loch was held back by a cofferdam, and the plan was to construct part of the rig and then flood this hole.

After flooding the cofferdam would be removed to allow for the structure would be floated. The structure was then to be towed into the deeper waters of the loch where the remainder of the work would be carried out.

At this point in time, I was sleeping in a tacky old caravan that had a leaking roof It was damp and uncomfortable. But choices were few and far between and I saw no alternative at the time,

I knew it was a temporary measure and so I stuck it out. We worked 12 hour shifts 7 days a week. Overtime was always available. This was primarily because although the money was good the labour force turnover was about 70% in the early days.

This was mainly due to the very harsh conditions not just the weather but also the fact that the bottom of the hole was always covered in at least 30-40cm of water and all of us had to wade through this all day long. And I mean *__ALL DAY LONG__*. But I would often work an extra 2-3 hours a day.

Sometimes you could step on a piece of steel that had dropped into the water. There were many injuries. There was trade union representation of sorts, but the construction was under the management of a company notorious in those days for not recognizing most unions except those they had in their pocket.

This today may sound a bit far-fetched but believe me that's how things were.

In fact, at one point there was some industrial dispute at the site and the old man himself - (Sir John Howard no less), flew in by helicopter from Dalcross Airport.

Within one hour of being on-site he gave orders for **every** man on strike to be **instantly** paid off.

He brought in fresh labour from his other sites all over the country and even though the gate had pickets in place for several weeks he never relented.

Eventually the dispute was settled and a few of those previously dismissed were re-employed - but only a few.

As I mentioned previously, times were tough in the Highlands of Scotland in the '70's.

In March of that year, I was lying in bed in the damp caravan feeling very poorly with a chest infection. Someone came to the caravan and told me there was an urgent message from my wife. I had to leave my bed and was taken to the office where there was a telephone.

I called June in Ardersier where we were living, and she passed on the news that my mum was critically ill in hospital.

I had not told June that I was sick but just told her to get Scott and herself ready, I would be there in a couple of hours. I got in my car and drove from Kishorn to Ardersier. Then the three of us got into the car and we drove through the night reaching the hospice in Rochester at around eight o'clock the following morning

We were able to see my mum and I spoke her before she died later the following morning, Saturday 13 March.

When she died it was as though a part of me had been taken literally from my soul. I shall never forget that feeling of emptiness.

Arrangements were made for mum's funeral and on the day before, my dad went into hospital, and he could not attend mum's funeral. Dad was obviously broken by mum's death. I could not bear the thought of my dad being left on his own especially as it was the first time in my life that I had seen him so vulnerable. He had always been a rock.

My sister lived up the road, and I thought she would take care of him as she was bringing up her own family in the village. But she could not.

My brother in Northfleet could not take care of him either for similar reason. Dad may have been OK on his own, but I was not happy about this at all. I discussed it with June, and we agreed that we would leave Ardersier in Scotland and come to Kent to live with Dad and see to him.

When he came out of hospital, and I suggested that we could come down to Higham to live with him. He was so happy with this idea.

Then we left Kent and drove back to Scotland promising Dad we would be back shortly.

Now back in Scotland, I called the company I was working for and told them I was not coming back. They were furious and told me that I should at least work my notice. But I did not and never did return to that awful place.

I rented a truck, loaded all our furniture and belongings myself, and the 3 of us drove the truck down to Kent. I offloaded the truck myself, had a sleep, and then I then drove the truck back up for the 12-hour drive to Ardersier.

I then rested for a few hours before returning the truck to the rental company.

I then collected my car, popped the house keys through the letter box, called the council office to tell them I was leaving and drove back down to Kent.

On the way down there were torrential rains all over the country and I was lucky to get out of **Pitlochry** with just minutes-to-spare before it was cut off by the floods.

That section of the A9 was cut off for the next 3 days. I was lucky to get through with just minutes to spare. But then I should not be surprised because God has always been there for me so many times and I didn't know it in those days.

It's funny how when I look back on some of the escapes, I've had from difficult situations I could never on my own have achieved the result. That was our Scotland experience over – or was it?

Taylors Lane

Now it was 1976. We four, June, Scott, Dad and I were at the council house that was built by German POWs at no 4 Taylors Lane.

My parents had been allocated this brand-new house 29 years earlier in 1947 and I lived in that house during much of my childhood.

These 14 pairs of houses were located between two roads, School Lane and Taylors Lane. The scheme had the grand name of *Mountbatten Estate* in honour of *Earl Mountbatten* who had previously been *Viceroy of India.*

Our house had 3 bedrooms and a proper bathroom. There was also a downstairs toilet in the attached lobby opposite the coal bunker. The heating was by a coal fire in the front living room and in the biggest of the 3 bedrooms.

After the small cottage at Lower Higham this was like *Buckingham Palace* to us. We had a huge garden that was never properly cultivated, and Dad grew what I believed to be the world's tastiest tomatoes.

These with cucumber we gathered from the green house that he had built himself. June and I set about decorating the house which had been a bit neglected because my parents were not able to do much of that sort of thing at their time if life. We got rid of some of the old furniture and replaced it with our newer stuff and bought a few extra bits and pieces.

We did this with the right spirit thinking it was the correct thing to do. But one thing we did not consider sufficiently was how my dad felt about the changes.

After all, this was his house, not ours and our tastes in many things were not necessarily his. At first all went well, and I got a job as a scaffolder at Littlebrook D power station.

Littlebrook

There were many labour strikes at the plant, and this always affected our take home pay.

Things got very tight and this is where we developed our expression *"living out of the tin".* This meant that on each pay day I would come home from work, and we would get out the old biscuit tin from the cupboard. There were no biscuits but if we were lucky there would be a few coins left over from last week.

In this tin were several envelopes each with its own label.

Rent, Gas, Electricity, Scott's Food, Scott's Nappies, Our Food, Petrol, Dinner Money. Etc.

This was how we lived then and there wasn't much for anything else really.

We might manage to go out perhaps on a Saturday evening to the working men's club or somewhere, but money was very tight. We scraped through though, and our son Scott, always came first. We made sure he never wanted for nourishment and most important our love and attention.

We had *nothing in the bank* and lived from pay day to pay day.

I even had to by-pass the electricity meter so we could keep the bills to a minimum. This of course was without the knowledge of my dad who would have been really upset had he known of it. But as I said, things were tight, and I had to take these risks to keep my family warm. June collected her family allowance for the baby (Scott) and there were times when this was all there was coming into the household from us 3 when the power station project was on strike.

My dad of course contributed what he could from his small pension, but we had little to spare. June and me together had dug up and cultivated that huge garden and we grew loads of vegetables.

We had wonderful crops of runner beans, cabbage, potatoes, and a few other vegetables. We had no joy with onions, and we had lots of laughs at ourselves in our endeavours trying to grow them. Our neighbours were so kind and helpful, and despite financial hardship, we were very happy there.

However, tensions within the house emerged between Dad and June at first and later I too became a player in the saga. It reached a point where I was almost violent with my dad and I knew at that point that we could not continue like this.

We had to find somewhere else to live. *And we did.*

My brother and sister had their own lives to live and I quietly resented them. They had their own valid reasons, but I could only see that they were not understanding the tense situation that had developed. And so, I did not confide in them anything about our intentions.

Our move to the Isle of Grain was not a very happy experience.

We told no one in the family of our plans until the day arrived for moving out of Taylor's Lane. My relationship with my brother **had reached a low point**.

I don't blame him for being hostile towards June and myself, but if he had known the true facts, he may have seen things very differently.

Anyway, we flitted one morning and that was that. I rented a truck and we moved ourselves. I had done the same before and moved my home 600 miles so moving my home around 20 miles away **was like a walk in the park.**

But having said that, it was a painful experience, and not the way I had hoped for when we moved everything from Scotland to Kent. But now we were at our new home, for which we had somehow obtained a mortgage.

I just had to be sure that my income was adequate and regular enough to sustain the payments.

The power station job was very much hit and miss for regular money because of the strikes.

I was getting fed up with these strikes that we're in fact working against us all. We were the losers and most of the men knew that in their heart of hearts.

But when a meeting was called to decide upon action to take, hardly anyone ever stood up to challenge the argument put forward by those calling for strike action. Just like lambs we followed the Judas sheep every time.

The irony of it was this. Those agitating for strike action could never be found on the picket lines. I discovered that many of them were away doing *"private works"* that they had already lined up for themselves before the strikes.

One of these fellows was a man in my own scaffolding unit. His name was **Terry B.** Terry was a bone-idle fellow who my colleagues and myself had protected many times before by covering up for his absences and his lack of effort. He was a great talker and that's all he seemed to do.........talk, talk, talk. His uncle was a notorious gangster who worked with the **Kray Twins,** who dominated the London underworld in the sixties.

And so, one day he was sacked for being unreliable and unproductive. In fact, it was a fair punishment and, should have been done long ago.

But as usual, he made a fuss of it all and a meeting was called. The result of the meeting was strike-action.

We were outside the gate for about 3 weeks. I was on that picket line day after day. In fact, it was me now acting like a sheep. Today I know that *I mistook my sheepishness for loyalty*.

Terry, meanwhile, and all through this strike, ***never once appeared on the picket line.*** I discovered he had a job in Stepney with ***"money in the hand".*** Meanwhile, my family was going without because we had no money coming in.

The irony was, that Terry got reinstated, and he was paid 3 weeks loss of pay for unlawful dismissal. The rest of us? Well, we were strikers, so we got NOTHING.

And so, one day when yet another call for strike action was being made, I was so fed up with this carry on, that went forward and took the microphone and challenged the agitators that were calling for strike action. (***I had done a similar thing on another occasion when I first went there but I was shouted down and called names by a lot of people in the crowd.***)

I was nervous that the same would happen again, but I had decided enough was enough. (There were over 3,000 men at the site at the height of construction.)

To my surprise many of the crowd supported me loudly. I don't recall if any decision on this occasion on strike action but shortly after the meeting I was approached by one of the shop stewards that I had a lot of respect for.

His name was ***Jack F.,*** and he asked me if he could put my name forward as a steward. I point blank refused saying I was totally fed up with the way things were and was considering leaving the job.

Although Jack was a paid-up member of the Communist Party, he was not an agitator, and he struck me as a very decent man who sacrificed his time fighting for justice and fair play. ***I had a lot of respect for him and his moderate views.***

After some discussion with Jack and several other moderate stewards they encouraged me to agree to allow myself to be put forward for election.

After the formalities were done through a couple of meetings of the work force, I was nominated and elected as shop steward for the scaffolding section of ***Gleeson*** workers.

Soon after I began my duties as steward, I was asked to be ***bonus-steward*** and took this on-board too. This was the turning point.

As bonus-steward, I met on a weekly basis with the company representatives consisting of the bonus Quantity Surveyor, the payroll manager, project engineer and a couple of others.

At the very first meeting, I detected that the Gleeson management were steamrolling their way through the discussions, trying to avoid details of how the bonus scheme was administered by them. Undeterred, I asked a lot of questions about the bonus scheme. After all, this scheme determined the size our pay at the end of each week.

Because I had previously done a little studying in QS activities I could tell when they were giving us a load of b.s. Additionally, and by doing some research in the public library during the evenings I quickly discovered that this bonus scheme was in fact illegal _**under the existing labour law at that time.**_

Slowly but surely, I raised this with top management and eventually the scheme was changed.

Our hourly rate rose *significantly*. When I started as bonus clerk the hourly bonus rate never exceeded 5 shillings an hour. (25 pence in today's money)

When I eventually left the company, we were earning an average of 12 times that amount even occasionally up to 4 pounds an hour bonus.

The hourly rate for my job then was something like 88 pence. The amazing thing was the company was happy because strikes became a thing of the past and the power station was getting built, targets were being met and the workforce was putting money in the bank for the first time.

I eventually decided to leave the company as *I had got a job offer in Kuwait.*

I gave in my notice and on my last day at the company two things happened that have remained clear in my memory.

Anyway, the project manager at the site was *Iain Lamon*t, the brother of MP Norman Lamont who later became Chancellor in the government of John Major.

Anyway, he sent someone down to the site and I was summoned to his office.

I went to his office, and he surprised me by *saying he was sorry to see me leaving.* This is spite of the fact that my tenacious actions towards the bonus scheme had been costing him a lot more money. I had never actually sat down with this man before and I was quite flabbergasted at his very civil attitude towards me.

He further went on to say that if things didn't work out for me in Kuwait, he would be happy to give me a job. *"But"*, he said, *"this time you'll come to my side of the firm"*.

I was flattered by this, but I'd had more than enough of the restrictive practices in UK that I thought stifled the growth of many individuals that were quite capable of more.

But the political system in UK at that time was not conducive to changes. That was to become different later – initiated in the main part by *Margaret Thatcher's* policies gravitating towards the so called *"free market economy"*.

But I'd better stop here, or I'll rant on forever.

The other thing that happened that same day was that a meeting was held during the lunch break and quite a lot of the lads came forward to shake my hand and wish me well on my new job. I was given three cheers which was a bit o.t.t. as I had only been doing my job as steward after all.

Then Jack F. who was now the *senior convener steward* for the whole of the project handed me a large envelope saying it was a token of appreciation from the lads.

The envelope was crammed full of money, many of five pounds, some of ten.. I was near to tears and in fact even remembering this as I write makes me feel a bit emotional. I still have the list of those men that donated towards this. There are 126 names on the paper.

CHAPTER 6 Kuwait

My plan was to work in Kuwait for one year and try to pay off the mortgage in that time. Then I planned to return to UK and "LIVE HAPPILY EVER AFTER". But not all plans work out the way we think.

Arriving at Kuwait airport I was expecting someone from the company to be there to meet me but there was no-one. The office was closed at the time I arrived, and I took a taxi and booked into the Hilton Hotel. The construction of the Kuwait Towers had recently been finished and my room overlooked them. These towers were later to become an icon for Kuwait after the invasion of 1990 by Iraqi forces.

On arrival, I was needing a drink and when I opened the mini bar in the room, guess what?...........Like old mother Hubbard and her cupboard, the mini bar was bare (of alcoholic beverages that is).

Undaunted, I called for room service. In a couple of minutes there was a gentle knock on the door. I opened it and politely requested the man to bring me a bottle of whisky. He (also politely) told me that alcohol was "haram" in Kuwait, even in the hotels. In those days Hilton hotels really were five-star, and I found it hard to believe that they could not serve a guest with booze.   I was shattered. I needed a drink and could not get to sleep without one for most of that night.

Next morning a car arrived at the hotel to take me to the office where I met the General Manager who welcomed me to *The Company.* I was a bit shaky and needed a drink but could not get anything. I don't think I created a very good first impression at all.

After meeting several other members of the staff, I was taken to *Shuaiba Port* to join the dredger I was to work on for the next several years.

The name of this dredge was *Mubarak*. It was named after one of the early Sheiks of the ruling *Al-Sabah* family.

At that time, *this was one of the most powerful cutter suction dredgers in the world.*

It had a full crew of around 65 people consisting of Master, Chief Engineer, dredge masters, engineers, welders, mechanics, divers, deckhands, skippers, surveyors etc. The captain and Chief Engineer plus other senior crew members were primarily from Holland.

From the start, some of these Dutch people made it difficult for me. The primary reason can be explained as follows. The company was tri-partite formation comprising two Kuwaiti partners and one Dutch partner.

The idea behind it all was that the Kuwait government of the day wanted to establish a Kuwaiti dredging company. To do this they enabled two local Kuwaiti companies to partner up and invited a Dutch company with international expertise in dredging and marine construction activities, to participate. Each partner would hold one third of the shares in *The Company*. All equipment and personnel would be sourced from overseas and the management of the company would initially be led from the front by the Dutch entity with the Kuwaiti partnership *"shadowing"*. The initial manning would be done using very experienced Dutch dredging personnel supported by experienced dredging personnel recruited from Singapore.

Part of the planning was for the senior positions held by the Dutch to be replaced by the newly recruited Brits. I was one just of those.

But the Dutch had their own hidden agenda and made sure that the transition would take as long as possible. To facilitate this, they would place obstacles in the way of the Brits.

Therefore, the transition period was substantially increased thereby providing the Dutch partners with continued control over the whole operations. In other words, they had outwitted the Kuwaitis when it came to the terms of the partnership.

One advantage (amongst others) would be for the purchasing of very expensive spare parts through The Company.

The Kuwaiti entity within The Company would pay for the parts and the Dutch entity would profit as the seller. It was a pretty good set up for the Dutch and no wonder they wanted to extend this arrangement for as long as possible. Who wouldn't?

Anyway, all good things do come to an end at some time and that time came for the Dutch partnership around 1981.

When the Dutch senior personnel left, I was eventually made *Captain* of the vessel and things worked out better - (for me at least).

We undertook several very profitable projects and although we had our share of setbacks, we managed quite well overall. In 1983 we had no work on the horizon, and we mothballed our fleet. I along with others was asked to go on long leave until we were able to get other projects.

I refused to do this without pay. I was told quite snottily by the personnel manager that all others were going to comply. I said to him that what others did was *none of my business.* The company either paid my salary or paid me off. I was uncompromising on this score.

So, much to the dismay of the personnel manager I was paid off with full indemnities.

Two months later they called me back. I was happy they called me back, *but when they offered me the same terms and conditions I refused.*

I knew it was a gamble, and they might offer the position to someone else, but I had to try to negotiate a better deal. In honesty, I knew I would be the loser if they refused as I could not now accept their offer. But I kept my nerve and opened negotiations with the management.

And luck was on my side once more and I negotiated a better deal. Only then did I return to Kuwait.

The other senior members of staff were unhappy that I had not only received my indemnities from the previous years of service but had returned on a higher salary and increased benefits.

This is where I discovered the *evil thread of jealousy* that can run through a group of *supposedly adult men*.

I have never been jealous of anyone to my knowledge, and it was a shock to me to find that instead of (some) of my colleagues being happy for me to secure an increase in salary etc. they were in fact working behind my back to undermine me. It went as far this.

One day I was called to the office to meet with the *Personnel Manager* only to be told that the car that the company provided me with had to be exchanged for a lesser grade model. I was astonished as I had negotiated into my contract that the company would provide me with a new minimum 2.8 litre automatic etc. Now they wanted me to downgrade to a 2.0 litre.

When I asked the reason, I was told that even the (Dutch) Chief Engineer in the company and the (Dutch) Senior Dredge-master were provided only with 2.0 litre vehicles and it was causing them discomfort when they saw the company was providing me with a 2.8 litre vehicle.

My response to all this nonsense was to remind the Personnel Manager *(a Kuwaiti)* that my contract was not negotiable and if *The Company* (i.e. the Personnel Manager himself) wished to appease these characters - **by raising their standards**, then I had no objection.

However, I would in no way *lower my standards* to theirs.

They negotiated their contracts, and they were happy enough with what they ended up with. I negotiated mine and that was that as far as I was concerned.

The guy was flabbergasted at my refusal as he expected me to comply. Now he was between *Scylla and Charybdis* and was very upset with me for not going along with it.

This was another incident that tested and stretched my already uncomfortable relationship with the *Personnel Manager.*

Marine Superintendent

By 1987 I was still working in Kuwait for the same company. I had risen to the position of Marine Superintendent, and at that time we had only a handful of small projects under way.

One of these projects involved the refurbishment of a small man-made island that had been constructed in the early 1950s. The island lay about 800 metres **offshore**, in shallow water, close to the Kuwait Ports communications tower near the *Seif Palace.*

The island's purpose was purely symbolic and protective. It marked and preserved the location of what was believed to be *the first offshore oil well in Kuwaiti waters*. The island fell under the control of the *Kuwait Oil Company (KOC),* and they had invited tenders for its restoration and refurbishment.

Our company submitted the lowest bid and was awarded the contract. I was appointed *Project Manager*. At *The Company,* titles were flexible—if you wanted to stay involved, you wore several hats at once. There were no restrictive practices, and I was used to that by then.

The scope of work was straightforward enough. It included demolition of the existing structures, construction of a new concrete platform, a small landing stage for boats, and two small buildings—one to house a rectifier room and the other a feeder pillar to supply electrical power for lighting on the island.

In addition, an 800-metre trench had to be dredged from the island back to shore. A power cable would be laid in the trench, which would then be backfilled. On paper, it was a simple job. The real problem was the price.

We had priced it **far too low**. It was obvious that the job had been taken on more for prestige than for profit.

One day in April, my **Managing Director** arrived on site and asked me to arrange for him to go offshore to inspect progress on the island. Unfortunately, his visit coincided with a particularly sensitive security window.

The project site was only metres away from where an assassination attempt had been made on **Sheikh Jaber Al-Ahmad Al-Jaber Al-Sabah**, the ruler of Kuwait, just months earlier. Since that incident, security in the area was heightened every day around noon—the time when the Sheikh's motorcade travelled from the **Seif Palace** to his residence at **Dasman.**

On that day, at the time of my MD's visit, the **Coast Guard** refused to grant me permission for any small craft to move in the area. I explained this to the MD as calmly as I could.

He responded by ranting at me and behaving arrogantly, as though I had **personally orchestrated** the security lockdown to inconvenience him. I listened for as long as I could tolerate, then simply walked away.

About ten minutes later, I received a call on the VHF radio informing me that permission had finally been granted by the **Coast Guard**. I called the boat in, and it came alongside the shore.

The Managing Director walked toward the boat, then turned and beckoned for me to join him. I told him—calmly—that he could go on his own. I said I was going home, and that he would receive my resignation the following morning.

I had truly had enough.

I got into my car and drove home. I explained everything to **June**. Then I sat down at my typewriter, typed out my resignation letter, and signed it.

The company accepted my resignation. After I worked my notice period, my indemnities were paid. We sold almost everything we owned in Kuwait, shipping only a few personal items back to the UK. And then we left Kuwait.

That chapter of my working life was over, - for now at least.

CHAPTER 7 Back In Uk

Arriving back in UK I convinced June that I was going to start a business in Scotland. No matter what I ever did or said, my June always had faith in me despite letting her down time after time.

But first I knew that I needed to acquire some I.T skills and so I enrolled for a course at the *Inverness College of Technology.*

On the first day of the course, I was up early and readied myself. I left the house neat and tidy, and June waved me off as I went down the road to the bus stop.

I turned up at the classroom on first morning with my little briefcase and was introduced to the course materials.

In my 47th year of life I was by far the eldest of all the students and even the tutor was about 15 years my junior. After about one hour I made an excuse and left the classroom. I was *craving a drink* and knew that the bars would be open just down the road from the college. *In those days the pubs opened at 9:00 am*

I hurried to the nearest bar and slugged down a couple of large ones. Then I bought a half bottle of vodka and scurried back to the classroom. Nobody said anything to me, and I would slip out of the classroom from time to time - (to the toilet), just to have a slug from the bottle.

I had no idea what was going on. I just knew I did not feel right in the classroom and the old feelings of *inadequacy and inferiority* were overwhelming at times. I was reminded of my unhappy school years and wanted to bury myself in self-pity and remorse. *I was not a happy camper*.

And so, the inevitable happened. I turned up at the college for the next couple of days and followed a similar routine from day one, - sliding in and out of the classroom *to top up* with booze.

All this did was to enhance my guilt and disgust with myself for being this way. But I could not stop. It was awful. I had by this time saved more than enough money to finance my boozing without having to keep June short of money, but this fact did not eliminate my feeling of guilt.

After a few days *I did not even bother going* to the college. Instead, I would leave the house as usual each morning and get the bus into town.

Then I would go into one of the bars and stay all day drinking before getting the bus back in the late afternoon.

I came in one afternoon the worse for wear and June knew I must have been drinking much of the day by my condition. We had a few words, and I told her the truth at last.

Well, it was my idea of truth. In fact, *just another lie.* I told her that the course had finished, and I celebrated with other students, hence my condition.

Again, I was feeling so guilty about my constant lying to my dear June. *The lies and deceit became a huge burden*, but I carried on doing it. I would never admit to the amount of alcohol I was consuming. In fact, looking back I doubt if I knew the amount myself. But it was far too much, and I could never be classed as *just a heavy drinker.*

I had gone past that point long ago. *My drinking was totally out of control*, and *so was I* for much of the time. My life had become truly unmanageable.

I got into several scrapes in pubs and clubs and hotel bars. I was arrested several times and taken to the cells to sober up.

I was charged and convicted with being drunk and disorderly on more than one occasion. All this in just a few weeks of being back in UK. I was just a pest to others and a poor husband and father. I just could not go on like this.

Then one day I was offered a good job in *Abu Dhabi*. The only condition was to turn up for an interview with the General Manager of the company. This guy was *Don R.* who was a British citizen. The arrangement was for me to go to *Brighton* in S.E. England for the interview.

The person who arranged all this for me was a friend called *Mike H.* and he told me something like this.

"The job is yours Dougie, but for Christ's sake don't take a drink before you go. That's all".

Mike and I were old drinking buddies, and he knew what I was like once I went on the booze, I simply could not stop.

So, I did not drink for three days prior to traveling down by train to London.

I must point out here that for me to stay away from the booze for a while required that I drank so much that I made myself ill. *I would then shake and rattle for a day or two* and only then would I be able to stop for a few days. *But the build up to make myself ill was essential or I would simple drink as usual.*

Sounds crazy I know, but for me that is how it was.

The plan was this: I would book a sleeper on the **Caledonian Express** from Inverness to London. I would then go down to Kent and stay with my friend Nobby and his family over the weekend. On the Monday morning, I was to get the train to Brighton and arrive in time for the interview.

Then after the interview, I would get the train back to London and then the overnight train, arriving back home on Tuesday morning. A perfect plan? Well, you will know by now how some of my best plans often turned out don't you?

After leaving my home in a taxi on that Friday evening in September 1987 I had one of my *"brilliant ideas"*.

I told the driver to pull over at the licenced grocer in **Telford Street.** I went in and bought two half bottles of whisky. I thought that this would help sustain me on the 11hour train journey to London.

After all, I deserved a little refreshment as *I had been teetotal for three days.* This was quite unusual for me - (to not drink at all for more than one or two days), *so I felt I deserved a reward.*

Arriving at the railway station the London train was waiting at the platform. There was still about 20 minutes before departure so after putting my bags in the sleeper compartment, I asked the **cabin attendant** to keep an eye on things whilst I went to find a toilet. (*Another lie;* I was going to the station bar).

After downing a few glasses, I returned to the train, and it shortly thereafter departed the station on the way to London.

As it was going to be a 11-hour journey I knew I would need a few extra drinks as the two half bottles I had purchased earlier were not going to be enough. So, I persuaded the car attendant to part many of the miniatures he had on the trolley. He protested that there would not be much left for other customers.

Full of the *"old patter"* I had the nerve to tell him everyone would be sleeping, and they would not want anything. Anyway, after much cajoling and humouring the guy, I managed to secure about 15 or 20 miniatures from him, and he put them all in a bag for me.

I had to promise him not to cause any problems and of course I gave my solemn word.

I did not use the sleeper cabin at all except to park my bag. Instead, I was sitting in the lounge with other travellers, and we had a bit of a party. I suppose I was boring everyone to death **with my usual solutions for every problem on the planet**, but that was typical of me when in full flow. (Or was it more like being in *full flight from reality?*)

I got off the train in the morning at Euston Station feeling tired, hung over, and more than a bit rough. All the booze had gone, and I badly needed a *"livener"*.

So, I got a cab to Covent Garden market and managed to get a porter to purchase a half bottle of whisky for me. I then went over to London Bridge station and caught the train to Gravesend in Kent.

Instead of calling my pal Nobby to pick me up and take me to his house, I went to a club that I used to frequent many years before. It was basically just a drinking and gambling den. *A real dump.* Anyway, I booked into a room and slept for a while with the help of some more booze.

In the late afternoon I came to and continued drinking. To cut a long story short, my pal Nobby had made a few inquiries and discovered where I was. He came over to the club and told me that June had called him and because I had not shown up to meet him as arranged, she was worried sick.

Eventually I did call her and tried to assure her I would be ok and would be back home on Tuesday morning as arranged. First, I would be at the interview on Monday, *secure the job and all would be well*. Nothing to worry about I told her.

I can't remember arriving in Brighton on the train, I was still heavily under the influence. I did get to the interview and remember being brash, cocky, and arrogant to those around me.

When I left, I knew without a shadow of a doubt that *I had blown it.* I remember sitting on the stony beach at Brighton feeling so ashamed and so sorry for myself. Several people came to me and asked if I was OK.

I don't really know what happened over the next few days. Where I went, whom I saw remains a mystery. Another one of my *many alcoholic blackouts.*

I remember being on *Kings Cross Station* in London. It was night-time and I was laying on the pavement in the station. I remember the police moving me on.

The next thing I know for sure is I was at my home in Inverness. It was Friday 11th September and not Tuesday 8th as planned. I had arrived in a cab from the railway station, and my June had to pay for it. *I was totally broken.*

I'd lost my briefcase and my overnight bag. My grey business- suit was filthy. I looked like a tramp. June was bewildered. She looked at me as though I was a stranger. I shall NEVER forget that look.

I could see it in her eyes. *"Who are you?"* It scared the hell out of me.

She just could not imagine how on earth I had left the house six days before, sober, clean, smartly dressed, confident, hopeful. I had now returned home in this condition. How had this happened?

She was as bewildered as I was, and I was gripped with a fear so awful that it bordered on terror. I knew that I had to do something about my drinking, but what that was I just didn't know.

June mentioned AA and somehow, I managed to call the help line. At least I think it was me that called. It may have been June.

The next morning (Saturday 12th September 1987), someone came to my house and *"12 stepped"* me. His name was *Billy* and he drove a Taxi for a living. He told me he had taken me to the airport once or twice in the past and *never* had me down as someone who had a drink problem.

He had the impression that I was a *successful businessman* or something like that. He never ever saw me the worse for drink.

Anyway, after listening to me for just a few minutes he said, *"oh yes, you sound very much like you are one of us"*. I later learned that he meant I was an "alcoholic" just like him and millions of others.

But those many millions, like him, had found a lifeline and a recovery programme in the fellowship of *Alcoholics Anonymous.*

That was the beginning of a new way of life for me that has continued up to the present day.

He took me to a meeting that night which was being held at the *local psychiatric hospital – Craig Dunain.*

I remember people being so kind and caring towards me, people I had never seen before. I was offered coffee and someone wisely *half-filled the cup* so that my shaky hands would not spill it everywhere and embarrass me.

I don't remember much about the meeting as I was still partly under the influence although I had only drunk a small amount during the day to *"settle my shakes"*.

At the end of the meeting, I remember people offering to take me home in their cars, but I refused, telling them I lived just a few minutes' walk away.

That was basically true, but the underlying reason was something else which I only learned about later when I began to live soberly. The main reason I did not accept the offers of a lift was that I did not want to *"obligate myself to anyone"* in case I might have to *"give something back"*.

I never wanted people to get too close to me. It might lead to me having to make a commitment to someone and I liked my independence too much. I later learned this had a lot to do with my, (yet unchecked), self-centredness.

I got back home from the meeting and was gasping for a drink. They had begged me at the meeting not to drink just for the rest of the day, but I could not. I had an 18-year-old bottle of The McCallan a rare single malt whisky. I was told recently that if I still had that same bottle of whisky, I could sell it for £3,500.00 at today's prices as it is a collector's item. Anyway, up until today, that was my last drink of alcohol.

Only much later, when I started to work the recovery programme, and to go through the steps, did it become clear to me that this was pure selfishness on my part. But that's a long story that might become clearer later.

Anyway, from that day forward I attended these AA meetings every day for one year. I never missed a day without going to a meeting. I made new friends amongst these people and *going to a meeting became the highlight of my day.*

I was now not ready to get back to full time work. I did not want anything to interfere with my ability to attend every meeting possible. And so, and I made an application for a *Private Hire Cab Licence* with the Highland Regional Council. This would allow me to choose my own hours and not be governed by terms and conditions of a contract of employment.

I succeeded with the licence, and I was able then to earn a little money and at the same time choose the hours I worked so it did not interfere with me getting to my AA meetings.

I was encouraged to look at the programme of recovery available to all of us in the fellowship. It was pointed out to me that *staying away from just one drink for one day at a time was fundamental.*

But to do this for a long period of time I would need something to satisfy me at least as much as drinking did - (at one time anyway).

During those early days of recovery, I experienced what is often termed as a *"Pink Cloud Experience".* This was a sensation that everything in the world was almost perfect and I was free at last from being chained to my alcohol *"friend"* who had evolved into becoming my *"jailer".*

I can remember clearly that day in my early weeks of sobriety when I was walking over *Ness Bridge* in the town and realised that I was holding my head up high and was able to look at people in the street and in the buses and cars passing by. I could look at them all in the eye without averting my eyes away as in the past.

I was no longer ashamed of being myself. I was truly set free from my past. What a wonderful gift this was.

There is a saying in the fellowship, and it has proven itself to me and countless others. That saying is *"Face Everything and Recover - The Truth Will Set You Free".*

I was soon to be drawn close to several members of AA and used to make it a priority to meet with some of them every day.

Then one day I had an offer of a job in Kent with a dredging company.

I mentioned this to Ross J. a friend of mine in A.A. and told him it was a good job offer but I was reluctant to take it. He knew why. He told me it was because I had become to feel so safe and secure in my current environment and did not want anything to change that lovely feeling. He was right, and I agreed with him.

But then he said something that I shall always remember and thank him for. He just said this.

"Dougie. God didn't get you sober to keep you chained to driving Private Hire Cabs. You have other things to do. Go and do them. It's what you are cut out for."

And he was dead right on this too. I shall always be grateful to Ross for his wisdom and encouragement. And so, I accepted the job offer.

Nash Dredging & Karen

The job with *Nash Dredging* involved overseeing the operation of a pumping plant and managing the fill area at *Queenborough, on the Isle of Sheppey.* Like most dredging work, it paid well, and the rota suited me perfectly—two weeks on site followed by a full week at home for rest and recuperation. It felt like a good balance, and for once, life seemed reasonably settled.

One day I received a phone call from my sister. She told me that my daughter **Karen** had been to her house and was asking if she could see me.

I need to explain something here. I hadn't seen Karen since she was a baby. The thought that she wanted to meet me filled me with a mixture of joy, fear, and disbelief. *She was now twenty-one years old.*

Our first meeting took place at my workplace in Queenborough. Karen arrived in her car to collect me and take me out. From the moment we started talking, we began—carefully—to get to know one another. She was a lovely young woman: intelligent, clear-minded, and strong-willed. I could see immediately that she knew who she was.

On one day when Karen was due to visit me at work, I received a call on the *AA helpline.* Someone was reaching out for help and needed to be seen without delay.

I asked my engineer aboard the plant to tell my daughter I would be delayed, then headed for my car to go to the address I'd been given. As I reached the car, Karen arrived. I explained quickly what had come up and told her I had to go and see someone in distress.

Without hesitation, she said she would come with me.

Up to that point, I hadn't explained to Karen that I was a recovering alcoholic. She knew I didn't drink—but little more than that.

We arrived at a terraced house in Queenborough and knocked on the door. A woman answered and told me it was her husband who needed help. I asked if Karen could come in with me, and she agreed.

We sat down in the lounge. The man came in and sat opposite us. I asked him how I could help, and he began to speak. He told me he needed to stop drinking—that it was destroying his life. He said he had tried everything to cut down or stop altogether, but nothing worked.

He was tearful. His wife joined in, explaining how his drinking was tearing apart their family and affecting their two children. They were both in their early thirties and clearly under enormous strain.

I followed suggestions in our literature on how to deal with those reaching out and allowed him to speak for as long as he wanted without interruption at all. I just listened carefully.

When he had finished it was my turn and I knew that if I was going to help this man, I had to be completely honest.

I shared with them what alcohol had done to me—how it had become the dominant force in my life, how it had taken relationships, work, dignity, and self-respect.

Karen sat quietly while I spoke about how my drinking had contributed to the breakdown of my marriage to her mother, and how she herself had been an innocent victim of it all. I did my best to keep my emotions in check, but it wasn't easy.

After a while, we left but before doing so I promised the man—his name was **Tom**—that I would collect him the following evening and take him to an *Alcoholics Anonymous* meeting.

The next evening, I took Tom to a meeting in **Maidstone** and introduced him to others who were in recovery. Over the following days, I took him to several different meetings so he could widen his circle and begin to build connections with people who understood exactly what he was going through. That was how others had helped me, and this was my chance to pass it on.

I eventually lost regular contact with Tom, but several years later I heard that he was still sober and getting on with his life.

That was enough for me. There are so many rewards in getting sober but passing on the message of hope and seeing others recover from a seemingly hopeless condition is priceless. And I often think to myself, *"I could have missed all of this".*

Back To Kuwait in 1989

It was about this time when I was contacted by the personnel manager of my old company in Kuwait. He asked me if I would be willing to return to Kuwait to get involved in a new project that the company had recently been awarded by the government.

I was delighted to be given the opportunity as I really missed Kuwait but could not let him think I was that keen.

So, I played the cat and mouse game to secure a contract for myself that I would be happy with.

It took several weeks of negotiating and my wife June thought I was taking it a bit close to the wire and the company would look elsewhere. On this occasion, I had more leverage to negotiate a better deal as I was in a good job in UK with long term prospects.

But it paid off and I was able to put in my notice with the company in UK (Nash Dredging). The day after I submitted my notice, the *Marine Superintendent* came to see me. He tried to persuade me to stay but my mind was made up. I wanted to return to Kuwait.

He asked me if I would not withdraw my resignation, could I at least extend my departure for a few weeks so that the people I was training in the operational techniques would have a bit more time with me.

Knowing that if I didn't stay a bit longer as requested, the company would be forced to bring in people from Holland to cover me, I agreed. I would rather see local Brits take my place than the Dutch.

And so, six weeks later than I had planned I departed for Kuwait

On arrival in Kuwait, I was made very welcome by the senior management and briefed on the details of the project a power station intake at *Al-Zour*.

I had negotiated a good deal with 3 business class air tickets per year and 3 months paid leave. (I got home every 90 days for one-month vacation). My salary and other fringe benefits were very good so all in all I was a happy camper.

The first thing I had to do was to contact another recovering alkie. I had obtained a single telephone number from the World Service office in New York.

I had also heard that someone in recovery was attending the services at the Holy Mother Cathedral in Kuwait City each Friday.

Ans so, on the first Friday afternoon since my return, I went to see for myself.

Arriving at the **Holy Mother Cathedral** facility I wandered around trying to contact someone in AA.

Having no luck with this after asking several people, I got tired and walked over to the nearby Sheraton Hotel and had some tea in the lobby lounge.

Leaving there I thought I'd give it another try and whilst wandering around in the church compound I came across **Joe.** Now Joe was from Goa in India, and he was a member of AA.

I was so happy to have met another AA member. He took me over to the palm tree where standing there was another person there. Her name was **Simone,** and she was from France.

She had been in recovery for about 2 years. Sometime later, another person came to join us. His name was **Fritz,** and he was from Holland. It was wonderful.

We had nowhere to sit and the only shelter from the sun was the palm tree. We had no preamble or any structure that I had been used to in UK but there was a spiritual connection between us four people. *I was no longer alone.*

We were no longer strangers in a strange land. We were fellows in recovery together. It was quite amazing. Our meeting lasted about 30 minutes, and we basically just exchanged chit chat but there was a singleness of purpose to it all. *Our recovery from alcoholism.*

Every Friday we gathered there - sometimes just two of us sometimes three and sometimes four. But we were there every Friday. It became the highlight of my week.

We spoke to *The Bishop Micalleff* and explained to him why we came to the church compound and what our primary purpose was. He was truly a very understanding gentleman and allowed us the use of a small room on a Friday afternoon. We purchased a window type A/C unit and made ourselves more comfortable.

Later in the year we were joined by another two members, *Bassam* from Kuwait, and *Jean* from Waterloo, Ontario, Canada.

With the help of Bassam, we introduced the AA recovery programme to the local psychiatric hospital in *Sulaibikhat*. At that time (1989) cell phones were a rarity and mostly we communicated by land line telephones. I had a pager which was useful if one of the other group members wanted to contact me.

We carried on like this until August 1990. That was when the Iraqis invaded Kuwait and overran the country in 36 hours. Then *everything changed.*

Invasion

It was Wednesday 1st August 1990, and I was as usual having my evening meal in the Sultan Centre restaurant in Salmiya. Because I used this place quite frequently, I had got to know several of the regular customers. One of these was a Kuwaiti fellow - (Ahmed), in his early 20's, who was a soldier in the Kuwait Army.

On this evening, he approached my table and asked if he could join me. I agreed, and we got chatting.

He told me that there was a massing of Iraqi troops at the border with Kuwait.

I had no prior knowledge of this and tried to assure him that it was probably just a scare tactic by Saddam Hussein to encourage the Kuwait leadership to toe his line.

I also told him that the British Government would not tolerate any kind of military incursion into Kuwait by Iraq or anyone else.

He seemed quite happy with my explanation, and we continued chatting whilst we ate our meal.

Earlier today I had received my air ticket for my upcoming leave scheduled to start in a few days. I was looking forward to sein my June and Scott again after several months here in Kuwait. But plans can sometimes be re-organised as I was soon to discover once again.

The next morning at around 04:30, I got out of my bed and went to the bathroom as usual. After showering I was getting my things together to go to my work when I heard an **unusual noise** from outside in the street.

It sounded as though planks of wood like scaffold boards were falling from the new building next door, which was under construction.

My apartment was on the 6th floor of the building and overlooked the big roundabout opposite the gate of the Dasman Palace. This palace is where the Emir of Kuwait spent most of his time during weekdays.

On this morning, looking from my window, I saw a Kuwait Transport Company (KTC) bus parked right across the main road. My impression was that there might be a VIP coming to visit the Emir and the police had blocked the road with the bus the control the traffic. **WRONG**.

Whilst looking out I heard the unusual noise again only this time louder. It was gunfire. Then I saw a soldier carrying a backpack with radio and long antenna, running across the parking lot opposite. This was where the *Kuwait State Security Building* was located.

My thoughts then were "it's a Coup d'état by the Kuwait army. They are going to raid the palace and capture the Emir". **WRONG AGAIN**.

I quickly picked up my briefcase and took the elevator to the lobby. One of the Philippine house-girls was at the reception counter and told me not to go outside. **"DANGER"** she yelled.

Being my usual self, I thanked her and went through the door to go to my car which was parked about 20 metres from the building.

After going down the few steps at the front of the building, I was overwhelmed by the sound of *heavy machine gun fire - very close by.*

With this, *I turned 180 degrees* and scurried back inside the building as fast as my legs would carry me.

I threw myself behind the reception desk where I discovered two of the house girls and another guest. This was my wake-up call. **DON'T LEAVE THE BUILDING.**

As I noted previously, directly opposite from where I was living was the *State Security Building* and this was obviously of interest to the soldiers who were attacking the building.

By 06:00 the residents in our building (awakened by the noise) were up and about - many of them gathering in the public areas on the ground floor. At about this time I managed to get a line to UK and woke June up to let her know what was happening.

She was upset but I told her not to worry as it would sort itself out. At that time, I still thought it might be a *Coup d'état.*

I spoke to a man that I had not seen before and asked him what he thought was happening. I knew it was a serious event but was not sure if it was a *Coup d'état* or invasion by outside forces. I asked him if he thought these were Kuwaiti soldiers running around outside.

Anyway, this gentleman with the *"Saddam Moustache"* just laughed. He mocked Kuwaiti soldiers saying something like.

"These Kuwaitis are like girls. Our guard will eat them. Now Kuwait is ours".

With that he just walked out of the building towards an armoured vehicle parked close by and spoke to some of the soldiers.

He was in civilian clothing but must have been a ranking officer in the Iraqi army or perhaps the Mahabharata judging by the reception he received from the soldiers. I never saw him again.

By about 10:00 am the noise of helicopters got my attention. I went out onto the roof and was shocked at what I was seeing.

As far as the eye could see, the sky was filled with helicopters. Some were gunships, others smaller. But there were many hundreds of them at various altitudes in the morning sky, I can't be sure of numbers but there were hundreds of them.

It was like looking at a war movie. It was totally surreal. It brought the hair on the back of my neck to attention I can tell you. It was hard to accept I was not dreaming all this. I have never seen anything like it, before or since.

In about another 45 minutes the sky had cleared substantially but there were still a few dozen choppers buzzing around all over the place. I assumed that many of these choppers had landed in various places to discharge the soldiers and others had gone further South.

At about 11:30 I decided to try my luck at making my way to the Corniche to see what was going on over there. I went outside and started my car waiting a little while to see if anyone would stop me. There were soldiers and tanks everywhere along the street, but no-one took any notice of me. So far so good I thought. Then I drove along and turned right which took me into the coast road.

As I drove along, I could see that a few r.p.g.'s had been fired at the famous **Kuwait Towers** landmark, but the damage was superficial with the main structures intact.

There were more soldiers in groups all along the Corniche and several tanks and armoured personnel carriers. The place was a real mess with paving stones having been ripped up where the tanks tracks had run over them.

The asphalt was damaged, and I needed to drive very slowly to avoid the debris.

I'd not gone too far, maybe 2 kilometres when I was flagged down by some soldiers.

I rolled down my window and tried to be cool. There was one soldier – a major who just looked at me without saying anything at first.

He came very close to my face and asked me who I was and where I was going.

I told him I was a British national working here and lived just along the road opposite the Sief palace. This man made me feel more than just a bit nervous. **He was scary.**

I guess he was about 28-30 years old at most, but looking at **his eyes** he was going on for 90 years of age. *They were the eyes of someone who had <u>seen everything,</u>* and it was quite a chilling experience to be near to him.

He was chewing on a toothpick in the corner of his mouth, and he said very quietly in perfect English. *"British, just turn your car around. Go back home and do not come here again".*

I gave him some kind of salute and said *"OK. You're the boss"* and did exactly what he told me to do.

Lucky for me no-one else stopped me on the way back and I parked up and went inside my building.

Sometime during the morning of that first day I witnessed something I'll never forget.

As I mentioned, the State Security building was opposite our building and from my room I had a clear view of the area. I looked out and saw two huge helicopters hovering above the parking area adjacent to the State Security building. I saw paratroopers from the Iraqi forces abseiling down from the choppers and surrounding the building.

From where I was situated, I could see over the compound wall and noticed some men stripping off their uniforms and putting on civilian clothes. These *were not* Iraqi soldiers.

These were the security forces of Kuwait that were supposed to be guarding the *State Security Building*.

One Iraqi soldier was approaching a hole in the wall where a tank had fired a shot making an opening in the perimeter wall.

As he got quite close there was some shouting from inside the compound and three of the State Security people (these ones had on their military uniforms) came through the hole in the wall putting their hands on their heads in surrender.

Not once did any of the security personnel I saw make any attempt to resist the invaders.

It seemed to justify the comment made earlier by the man with the Saddam moustache *"These Kuwaitis are like girls. Our guards will eat them......"*

I didn't try to leave the building for the rest of that first day as the *face of the Iraqi major* was a vivid reminder that I was lucky not to have been taken prisoner and sent to Iraq.

During the first few days I could move around somewhat using my rental car but had to be careful at intersections where the Iraqi's had checkpoints.

Being a British citizen, I was soon high on the list of expatriates that the Iraqi's wanted in their custody.

This was mainly due to our prime minister of the day - *(Margaret Thatcher)*, doing what she had to do and encouraging other world leaders to support the initiative she had started with **George Bush Snr.** on the very same day of the invasion to rally around together and kick Saddam and his army out of Kuwait.

After a few more days I was unable to move around and was confined to my lodgings and keeping out of sight. Even if I had been able to go out on the street, I would be restricted because *someone stole my car.*

The other people in my building consisted mainly of Asians and me being a white skinned Englishman I stood out like a sore thumb.

The Iraqi's were, at this time, threatening anyone harbouring or hiding British citizens with severe punishment if caught.

In fact, they did execute a man in Sharq *and hung his body high up on the hook of a mobile crane* for all to see.

The other residents in my building were very nervous of this and so afraid I would be caught, and they might be accused of harbouring me.

One man from Bahrain who worked for Kuwait Television pleaded with me not to go outside in case I was spotted.

Shortly after, I went to another nearby building to see if I could contact other Brits or Americans. The building was about 16 storeys and there were British families housed there.

I spoke to a man who was in the reception area, and he was a Brit named Bob B. He was a team leader of a group of people from UK who were responsible for the maintenance and operation of the **Doha East Power Station.**

He invited me upstairs to meet some of the others. There were families and children amongst this group. They were planning a gathering in one of these large apartments for that same evening and I was invited.

I thanked them and returned later that evening. We had turkey and all the trimmings. It was just lovely. They had some wine and I had to use my old favourite excuse for not taking any alcohol - *("thanks for the offer but I'm allergic to alcohol.")*

When it was time for me to go over to my own building I was advised to stay where I was as the Iraqi's were patrolling outside and around our buildings.

And so, I was given the keys to a fully equipped 4-bedroom apartment which was rented to one of the technicians who currently was on leave in UK. He would of course not be coming back soon, owing to these circumstances.

I could not move out of the building for about 6 days.

When I did get back to my apartment in the other building I was in for a shock. The building was now completely empty of people. There was no power at all and of course the elevators could not work. I had to walk up 6 floors to my little studio apartment.

When I got to my room the door was open. The place had been thoroughly trashed.

All my stuff had gone. Only thousands of cockroaches were crawling everywhere it was disgusting. It was astonishing that in just those six days the building where I had been living comfortably had been transformed into a filthy, cockroach-infested slum. I now had no choice but to move to the other building.

Because the power station at Doha which was the primary supplier of electricity to our area, was operating spasmodically due to lack of technical support, we were suffering because our power was only available for about 4 hours a day now.

Luckily for us, my new friends were all technicians in Power Supply and working together in shifts because of the head and security risks, we managed to rig a cable from the emergency generator from the now abandoned tower block nearby, to our own building. It was like being in heaven when at last we cranked up the genny and power was restored. The elevators now worked and best of all the fridge freezes and the AC units were back in action. It was August and the outside temperatures reached over 50 degrees Celsius.

We managed to get some food and pooled our resources. We were helped in this respect by some wonderful **Indian friends** who could move around freely.

They risked their own safety to help us.

I recall the time when I was in hiding and noticed there was blood in my urine. I developed a high temperature and needed medical support. But although the Amiri hospital was within walking distance I was afraid to go there in case I was captured.

One of these Indian friends risked bringing me antibiotics and additional medication from the hospital and I recovered. And again, *when I was able to contact the British Embassy for help, the negativity from the staff was appalling. They were just clueless.*

These Indian friends of our community are the people who should have been honoured after the liberation of Kuwait. They took enormous risks to help us.

Instead, honours were bestowed on people like the British ambassador*)*, and the likes who were in fact **a total disgrace** in the way they behaved towards the trapped British community. They did absolutely nothing to help us.

I remember taking a friend of mine and Armenian gentleman to the Embassy during the crisis. I sought help for him, but the senior embassy staff were nowhere to be found.

Instead, everything was left to junior staff to muddle through, and they lacked the necessary qualifications and authority to decide. It was another disgraceful example of an incompetent **Foreign Office.**

All we ever got from the Embassy when we managed to get through on the phone was a recorded message advising us to stay in hiding. It was something like, *"stay where you are and listen to the BBC for advice from the Foreign Office".*

The Canadian embassy on the other hand was so helpful.

We all agreed (those of us in hiding) that if we ever got out of Kuwait, we would take this issue up to the highest authorities.

But of course, when the ambassador and some of the others were later publicly acknowledged to be heroes of some sort or another, our chances of the truth being told was flattened.

On 4th September 1990, the Iraqi's allowed our women and children to leave. It was sad to see them go but also a relief to know that they would be safe in UK in a day or two. It was just about the best birthday present I could have had – (under the circumstances).

Each day we would meet and discuss our situation. It was impossible for us to move far as the whole country was under the control of the Iraqi forces. Some days we would have to hide when the Mahabharata were around. These were the *"secret police"* of the Saddam regime.

Some of us would hide away in the air conditioning ducting when these raids took place. Others might hide on the roof in empty freshwater storage tanks.

Everyone was really scared of these people. They were a law unto themselves.

A *Mahabharata* could summarily kill a citizen without any reason and could not be punished. Such was their power.

One day in September, a lot of noise emanating from several floors below got my attention. As we were always wary of being seen, I quietly made my way down the stairwell to investigate.

On reaching the ground floor I was confronted by several young **Palestinian men** who were carrying furniture and other property from various apartments and loading it all onto a large twelve-metre flatbed truck outside the building.

One of these guys was lounging on one of the armchairs in the foyer and I went over to him. I greeted him in the traditional Arabic ways and then asked him what was going on.

He told me they were taking the furniture and belongings of *"friends"*.

I knew this to be untrue as **ALL** this building had been let out to British employees of the company looking after the power stations in the country. And so, I politely challenged him about it.

He was quite adamant at first it was the property of *"friends"*, but when I pushed it further, he admitted they were looting the place because most of the residents had fled the country.

He said they would never return and so they could take anything left.

I asked him where his father was (he was about twenty-two years old I guess), and he told me his father was in Hawally – a district in Kuwait where *about four-hundred-thousand Palestinians lived at that time.*

I asked him if his father knew what he was doing. He answered yes.

I asked him where he had received his education. He said in Kuwait. I asked him where he was born. He said Kuwait.

I challenged him that if Kuwait had been his home and had provided him with an education and security, why was he behaving like this in such a callous way.

He said that Kuwait is going to be the 13th province of Iraq and that Saddam Hussein has promised *Yasser Arafat* that the Palestinian people would be the number one citizens of Kuwait and that all Kuwaitis would become second class citizens.

I pointed out to him that the rest of the world would not allow Kuwait to be occupied for too long and already measures were being taken by UN to gather support for kicking the Iraqis out of Kuwait.

He just got angry and told me that would never happen, and Kuwait was now a part of Iraq forever. I wondered at this point if it was this fellow and his gang of thieves who'd ransacked my building and stolen all my possessions including my car. But it could also have been others as there were many groups doing the same things.

Unfortunately, this was the attitude of many Palestinians who had lived and worked in Kuwait for many years.

Even *Yasser Arafat,* the - (then) leader of the PLO - (Palestine Liberation Organisation), was educated in Kuwait and in fact worked there for many years *as an electrical engineer*, before becoming a fugitive and rising through the ranks of the PLO.

But not all the looting was done by the Palestinians. There were trucks coming into Kuwait from Iraq every day, and returning to Iraq loaded with goods and booty.

The gold souk was looted, and the gold bullion reserves held by Kuwait Banks were also stolen by the Iraqi Army and sent to Iraq.

HOSTAGE

During the period I was hiding we all found various places within the building where we would hide away from the Iraqi soldiers that would often enter the building and snoop around.

On 4th October, two of our people in hiding were caught. They were taken away by the Iraqis. That evening we had a phone call from one of those that were captured.

He said that one of the secret police officers had let slip that the Kuwaiti resistance was going to kill some of the Brits in hiding and blame it on the Iraqis. In this way, the Kuwaitis figured that the UK government would be more inclined to take action to liberate the country.

Of course, we were all shocked at this statement and held an urgent meeting amongst ourselves to decide how we would react. There was plausibility in the threat as we knew how the resistance was so frustrated that the UN was against military action at that point in time.

As our meeting progressed, a couple of the men said it would be better to give ourselves up to the Iraqis. Another group advocated moving to a different building. And so, our discussions went on for most of that night.

My own opinion was not to move as I reasoned that although they had caught two of our group, the rest of us had remained free. My view was that the Iraqis were bluffing by making up a story about the Kuwait resistance and wanted us to turn ourselves in.

But by a majority, a decision was made to move to a safe house about 6 miles away. I said I was not going, and another guy said he would also stay put.

The remaining group planned to move out on the 7th of October.

On 6th October our building was raided by the **Mukhabarat.** I was able to hide for a while but then they found me. In fact, they found all of us.

We were all taken to the Hyatt Regency hotel and given some good food, the best we had eaten for weeks. The Hyatt was the headquarters of the Mukhabarat, and they had the best of everything.

We were kept there for one night only and then put on a bus the next day and taken on the long road journey to Baghdad.

When we reached there, we were put up at the Mansour Melia Hotel overnight and the next evening I was placed in a blacked-out Toyota 4wd and driven for about 2 hours to an unknown destination.

I later learned that I was now in Fallujah in Iraq and kept as a "Guest" of Saddam Hussein's government.

My new "home" was a factory that we came to understand was for the manufacture of chlorine, bleach, and other products. At least that is what we are told. The strange thing was that below ground there was a nuclear bomb shelter.

This was amazing, because it had (almost) everything needed to house many people for an indefinite period.

There were power generators, sophisticated air filtering systems, water storage tanks, even a reverse osmosis plant. It was huge and the entrance to it was through a massive steel door of circular design like those we see in space movies.

All this was built by East German engineers who (during the construction) had been housed in a purpose-built compound adjacent to the factory itself.

Our sleeping arrangements were bunk beds in the administrative office building of the factory.

We were not allowed outside but we did have free access (at first) to the underground nuclear bomb shelter.

Later, this freedom was denied us when we began to make comments on how the maintenance of the shelter needed to be done on a regular basis. There were 12 of us held as hostages (guests) in this facility:

NAME	NATIONALITY	PROFESSION	AGE
William Douglas	British	Dredge Master (G.D.C.)	50
Nick B.	British	Airline Pilot (Kuwait Airways)	43
Frank G.	British	Technician (B.E.C.)	43
Tony R.	British	Structural Engineer (Palace Project)	41
Les R.	British	Soldier (British Army- (Undercover)	34
Frank M.	French	Radar Technician (Thompson)	25
Wolfgang G.	German	Mechanical Engineer (Mercedes Benz)	38
Bernard K.	German	Civil Engineer (Seimens)	38
Dr. Clem H.	American	US Embassy Staff (Undercover)	36
Yutaka T.	Japanese	Project Director (Mitsui)	38
Hideo M.	Japanese	Project Manager (Mitsui)	37
Nick F.	Aussie,Irish,British	HVAC Engineer (M.E.W.)	49

Amongst our team were engineers and professionals of several descriptions and we could see that if the shelter was to be used in earnest, then many preparations were needed to ensure the survival of its occupants.

But the Iraqis were having none of it and we got the message loud and clear, *mind your own business.*

The treatment we received was not unkind but there was very little food. For example, if we ever had meat on the plate - (very rarely), it was a tiny amount, virtually one mouthful, never more than that - no kidding.

Our diet consisted mainly of bread and vegetables, mainly aubergines. I cannot eat aubergine today. The Iraq experience made aubergine my personal *food enemy number 1.*

As is my nature, I complained to the Iraqis about the facility we were being held at and the lack of proper and adequate food.

We had two Iraqi fellows who were designated interpreters for our group of 12. Between the two of them they covered the English, French, Japanese, German languages adequately.

There was Peter (a Christian) who was a very good-natured fellow in his mid-twenties and Saad (a Moslem) about the same age as Peter, also a very decent fellow.

One day, when I was complaining to Peter about the lack of proper nourishment we were getting, he suggested I write a letter to *"His Excellency the President"* noting down my complaints.

I was quite astonished at this suggestion and of course, I did not believe it would do any good if I did write as I believed it would never get anywhere past the security people.

But out of sheer frustration I wrote a polite letter and addressed it for the attention of *His Excellency Saddam Hussein President of The Iraqi Republic.*

I pointed out that if he really wanted to convince the world that we were *"Guests"* and not *"Human Shields"* let him show this by deed and actions.

I showed the letter to the other "inmates", and they all agreed to support it by adding their own signatures.

Only Tony R. had one comment. He was wanting it to go to *Tarek Aziz* who was the *Iraqi Foreign Minister*, but I insisted we start at the top and the others agreed.

Unbelievably, the letter was delivered, ***and not just delivered, but acted upon.***

Two days after I sent it via one of the Iraqi interpreters, who were with us at the facility, we were moved into a different environment.

This turned out to be the purpose-built compound that the German engineers had used during construction. It was remarkably different. We were now given good food including breakfast cereals and fresh fruit.

We were allowed to walk around freely inside the gated compound and enjoy other such freedoms we had not had previously.

I even had the luxury of a room to myself. (There was just one single occupancy room which everyone wanted, and we cut the cards to see who got it).

They gave us reading materials and newspapers.

On the second day in the new location, we were visited by some very senior officials of the Iraqi government including the **Vice President himself, Ezzat Ibrahim Al Nouri**. (This man was never captured as was Saddam, and he later became one of the leaders and founders of the so-called **Islamic State (ISIS or DAESH).**

We also had correspondents from Reuters - *(Subhy Haddad)* and Associated Press *(Salah Nasrawi).*

We could voice our concerns to the correspondents without any coercion by the guards.

I came to know later that they had pushed information of this visit out to the world media, but it was deemed as a propaganda item by Western governments and largely suppressed as a worthy news-item.

During the period of my internment by the Iraqi government I kept up my journaling a habit of many years, which has helped me to record with accuracy some of the events that took place.

We adopted a stray dog that had made the compound his home and this dog was so helpful to us all in several ways. He was not very old, perhaps a year or two and he was a delight to have around. We called him **SLOPPY.**

He would always chase after Nick F. when Nick was doing his walking exercises, and Nick used to get annoyed with him. The more he got annoyed, the more Sloppy would pester him.

One afternoon, as Nick was jogging along, Sloppy chasing at his heels, jumped up and grabbed the leg of his shorts. These were the type of shorts we wore in my schooldays for football and PT. Anyway, Nick was yelling at Sloppy when suddenly his shorts were pulled right down. It was hilarious to see. There was Nick without any underwear his big white bum *shining like a shilling in the sun..*

We were all in stitches watching this with Nick frantically trying to retrieve his shorts from Sloppy. It still makes me chuckle even today after all these years. I wonder where Nick is now.

Nick was a real character and its worth mentioning this about him. He was born in 1941 in England of Irish parents and in the 1950's he took an assisted passage and emigrated to Australia for just ten pounds. (£10.00)

Now this meant that Nick had 3 passports, British, Irish, Australian.

When he was captured in Kuwait, he claimed to be Irish, showing the Iraqi soldiers his Irish passport. As the Irish nationals were not on the hit list for being interned, he almost got away with it.

Unfortunately for him, whilst they were searching in his stuff, his other two passports came to light and the game was up. And so, he was treated as a Brit, joining the many other Brits including myself who had been detained.

In fact, when I eventually returned to Iraq in 1991 after the country had been liberated, I met Nick again on a power station project we were engaged on in Subiya in North of Kuwait.

He was there as an Irish citizen employed by the Kuwait Ministry of Electricity and Water (M.E.W.)

This time and told me he had burned his British passport as it gave him too much grief in the past.

He said it was safer to work as an Irish National than a Brit or Australian as both these counties were always poking their noses in other people's businesses.

Maybe he had a *valid point.*

Much of my time was spent reading, *writing my journal,* playing solitaire, playing scrabble or chess, with the other Brits, walking around the compound or sleeping.

One of the German fellows (Wolfgang) had a small radio that he'd managed to keep hidden from the guards. He was our source of international information on what was happening in the outside world.

Having said that, we did have access every day to the Baghdad Times Newspaper in English language but most of it was propagandist and heavily censored.

And so, naturally, Wolfgang was given the nickname of *"Radio Wolf"*.

Several times a day, he would appear amongst us with a bit of news from BBC, Voice of America, Radio Deutchavela, or one of the several stations he could pick up.

At this time - (1990), all these broadcasters would be using short wave frequencies, and the reception was always hit and miss. But we did get the news, and this too had its ups and downs.

For example, one minute it would be announced on say BBC that Saddam had agreed to comply with UN resolutions, and we all became elated, thinking we would soon be released.

Then an hour later, VOA would perhaps announce that Saddam had changes his mind and wanted sanctions lifted etc. Then our emotions took the opposite tack and bouts of depression became rife amongst some of the hostages.

One minute we were up, the next we were down. This could happen several times in just 24 hours, and it was hard to take.

Poor old Wolfgang got the brunt of our frustrations. He was just the messenger, but you know how it is when people are frustrated. They want to shoot the messenger.

One day, he came up with an idea.............

As he knew that the letter, I had written to Saddam Hussein had got results for us, he wrote one himself to Saddam citing the injustice of the UN sanctions on

Iraq which in his words, had the children of Iraq suffering because they could not get proper medical supplies and in particular babies' milk. He asked me if it would be okay with the group if he sent the letter. I suggested he ask each of them to see how it went, but as far as I was concerned to *"go for it."*

This letter in fact was published in the Baghdad Times English paper and translated for entry into the Arabic version.

Two days later, by *"Presidential Decree",* Wolfgang was taken from the camp, crossed the border into Jordan and put on a plane to Frankfurt, arriving the same day. And that is the story of our dear friend *"Radio Wolf".*

But before he left, he donated his precious short-wave radio set to our group of prisoners so we might continue to get the news from outside Iraq. This was so useful to us in many ways.

We did stay connected by mail and telephone for about 2 years after my own release, but we have since lost touch. I really did like this guy. A real character.

During the period, the **BBC** broadcast I think 2 times each week, a programme directed at the hostages and their families in UK. The name of this programme was *"Gulf Link"* and it was very popular.

Friends and families of the hostages were invited by the BBC to send in short, recorded messages which could be relayed over the airwaves to their loved ones in captivity.

We all used to huddle around the radio whenever this programme was on and would quite often hear a message from the family of someone we had known in Kuwait. One day, this message came over the air.:

"Hi Doug. This is a message from all your friends at the Raigmore Hospital Group in Inverness. We know that you are safe somewhere in Iraq and we want you to know that we are thinking of you and know we shall see you amongst us again. God be with you".

The message was sent by my pal **Don N.** who was also a member of the Raigmore Hospital AA group. Don and I became firm friends over several years - through our common problem, and we remained that way until he passed away in May 2004.

The message did not break my anonymity as no-one listening in could have any idea what kind of group Don was referring to. But I knew of course, and it lifted my spirits tremendously.

My lovely June tried and tried to get a message to me by the same way, but she was never lucky enough to have her message selected by the programme administrators. Obviously, only a few were lucky enough out of the probable hundreds who tried to send a message to their friends or relations in captivity.

Another one of the reluctant *"Guests of Saddam"* was Nick B.

I quite liked a lot of things about Nick, but he was a bit snobbish really, and he hated me beating him at chess and even the word game of Scrabble.

Not once in all the games we played did he ever beat me. Not that I am a brilliant player at all. Just that he was *never* able to beat me.

With him being university educated and me leaving school at 14 never did his ego much good. He just could not understand it at all. It must have been so painful for him, and it showed- especially each time he lost to me.

About influential politicians, and those that made independent efforts to get the British Hostages freed, I must mention here those that tried and some who got a measure of success.

There was *Ted Heath* for example, the former Prime Minister of UK, who came to Baghdad, met Saddam Hussein and went home with 30 or more ex-hostages on his flight.

What disgusted me and many others was that as soon as his plane landed at Heathrow, there were officials from the British government - (The Parliamentary Under-Secretary of State for Foreign and Commonwealth Affairs *(Mr. Mark Lennox-Boyd)* trying to take credit for Teds independent action.

In fact, the press tried to crucify him for going against the then government policy of not making any independent moves with Iraqi authorities.

The same type of vilification from government members and the mainstream media was meted out to others. They included *Tony Benn, George Galloway*, and several others who took real actions to free British hostages.

Muhammad Ali the ex-world heavyweight champion boxer went to Baghdad and took 15 American hostages' home with him. *Reverend Jesse Jackson* also took over 50 American with him after going to Baghdad and pleading with Saddam Hussein to release them on humanitarian grounds.

The facts of the matter are that the **real motives** behind the American and the British governments desire to invade Iraq *(in order to control the oil in the Middle East region),* were enhanced if the hostages remained as hostages. Remained at least until the mobilisation of the military were in place for expelling Iraqi troops from Kuwait.

The *"hawks"* in both administrations- (and that includes *George Bush* the US president at the time), really did not want to stop at expelling the Iraqis from Kuwait. There were those that wanted to occupy Iraq and take control over the middle east oil production capabilities. *I personally believe that this was the true motive* and not the humanitarian liberation of an occupied country as the press had convinced the populations of USA and UK.

If it had not been for the fact that *General Norman Schwarzkopf* (who was the commander of the coalition forces) had strongly advised the US President that the invasion of Iraq would be folly, then I personally believe the invasion of Iraq would have taken place in 1991.

Instead, it was the US president's son – *George W. Bush*, who along with the UK Prime Minister *Tony Blair*, who unilaterally invaded Iraq 13 years later, this time without United Nations approvals. It was later proven that the main pretext to invade Iraq was the fear of a nuclear arsenal that Saddam had developed. And indeed, it was just that, - **a pretext that so many of the citizens of USA and UK believed to be true.**

But thank heavens too that there were also many that did not believe such rubbish.

Anyone with *half a brain* would have known this could not be even remotely possible since the USA and UK air forces had been overflying Iraq daily since 1991.

Whilst I was living in Kuwait during the period from 1991 to 1998 I saw reports almost daily in the Arab press about UK and US Phantom fighter jets bombing anything that moved in Iraq that looked suspicious.

And because of that ***illegal*** invasion we all know what a mess this has got the world into. And ***Blair and Bush*** are still saying they were right. What a mess. But more about this later.

BRITISH EMBASSY AND F.C.O.

Here I must make a comment or two on the general behaviour the Foreign and Commonwealth Office and the British Embassy during this time of National Crisis.

As can be expected, when the invasion occurred, there was uncertainty and confusion amongst the whole of the population.

At the time there were several thousands of British Expatriates living and working in Kuwait. Some, like me had been here for a few years. Others newly arrived. But everyone was reaching out to the Embassy for advice and support.

The results were a great disappointment for everyone I know in the community - and I mean EVERONE.

After the liberation of Kuwait in 1991 I was in touch with many of the Brits who were in a similar position to me during the occupation of Kuwait by Iraqi forces.

Not even one of these Brits had a good word to say about the conduct towards the expat community from either the Foreign and Commonwealth Office (FCO) or the Embassy staff including the Ambassador at the time - Mike W.

This guy became a "hero" for doing nothing and was "KNIGHTED" by our queen. *"Sir Mike"* indeed.

This farce made many of us so angry when we knew how little he did for those in need of help at the time.

RELEASE FROM CAPTIVITY

On 9th December, we were informed by our captors that we were to be released and sent back to UK. On this news, we were of course excited at the prospect.

However, had we not heard this so many times in the past weeks only to have our hopes dashed shortly afterwards?

Yes, of course we had. And for that reason, I did not really expect it would happen. I was not alone with this same thought either. Some of the others were thinking the same.

But this was one occasion I was so happy to be wrong, because late in the evening we were told to collect our bits and pieces and be ready to move.

We were sent to the **Mansour Melia Hotel** in Baghdad prior to being released and repatriated to UK.

The Iraqis loaded us all into vehicles and we were delivered to the hotel arriving during the late evening of 9th December 1990.

On entering the huge hotel reception area, we were greeted by members of the FCO who were handing each person a bottle of **Johnnie Walker whisk**y plus a carton of **Benson & Hedges cigarettes.**

I accepted the cigarettes but refused the whisky and went over to where the then British Ambassador to Iraq – (**Sir Harold Walker**) was talking to a group of journalists.

At the first opportunity, I asked him point blank if it was wise to his staff members to hand out booze to innocent men who had been unlawfully locked up and deprived of their freedom at this sensitive time.

My reasons were based upon the undeniable fact that right now many of us were quite emotional at the prospect of being reunited with our families and I was conscious of the fact that booze coupled with highly emotive people could lead to trouble.

He - (**Sir Harold)**, was very condescending and told me not to worry. Besides he said, these were gifts from the UK citizens and **had to be distributed**. And this fellow went on to be bestowed the honour of **Knight Commander of the Order of St Michael and St George (KCMG)** by our queen. Is this another example of cronyism from **"The Establishment"**.

The **"wisdom"** of the statement from Sir Harold proved to be just an optimistic hope as trouble because drunken behaviour did break out during the next few hours.

It was fortunate for us that the Iraqi **Mukhabarata** who were mingling with the released expats kept their cool otherwise it could have been a different story.

We were eventually provided with a place to sleep for the night with a promise that the following day we would be repatriated by air to UK.

I could not sleep and went down into the atrium area where there were perhaps 200 people milling around, drinking, smoking, chatting.

I saw *Frank G.* who I had been locked up with in *Fallujah,* and we continued chatting away at the prospect of being free very soon and getting to see our families who we had not seen for months.

Looking around, I spotted a fellow - (who shall remain anonymous), that used to come to the Ray of Hope Group in Kuwait. He was a banker who visited us several times each year and had been to our meetings over a period of several years.

I must have let out a yell because my friend looked at me and said, **"is that one of your special friends?"** (I had previously broken my anonymity to Frank about me being a member of Alcoholics Anonymous).

I simply excused myself to go over to see the guy. I was very excited.

My joy to see him was shattered when, reaching to within about 6-8 feet from him, I could tell he was drunk. He looked at me and looked away as if he had never seen me before in his life.

I was mortified. I could not believe he would have picked up a drink. I was that naïve having convinced myself that ANYONE who practised the recovery programme to the best of their ability could not pick up a drink.

Since those days, I have learned so much and although it's sad to say I truly do accept the premise that *my own sobriety is contingent upon my spiritual condition* and not much else. If my spiritual condition is unhealthy then so is my sobriety at risk. I am convinced that my alcoholism has been arrested *but I am not cured.*

I could not sleep that night and I don't think many others did either. We were hyper. The next morning the buses came, and we were taken to the airport in Baghdad.

Iraqi Airways had prepared a 747 to take us back to UK. They would not allow any of the British or other foreign airlines to do this. The 747 had been prepared in such a way that all the bulkheads that divide the classes had been removed and we all were *"economy class"* only. **I would not have minded if it was standing room only.** I was just happy to be one of those 430 hostages onboard that *"jumbo".*

When we got onboard our passports were returned to us. Then it was down the runway and up into the clouds.

I had a seat next to **Nick B.** and he flew this type of aircraft for **Kuwait Airways,** so he knew a lot about them of course. After about 3 hours from Baghdad, he asked the purser if he could use the communications system to make an announcement to all of us. The purser was a decent fellow and asked the Iraqi pilot - who agreed.

Nick then announced to everyone onboard that because we now had used a certain quantity of aviation fuel, we did not have enough to return to Baghdad.

A huge cheer when up throughout the whole of the aircraft. Even up to that point we were not convinced that something would happen to change the orders and we would have to go back. I shall never forget that moment. It was such an emotional experience for us all. *Even the Iraqi flight crew seemed delighted for us.*

Arriving at **Gatwick,** there were of course dozens of journalists, and *paparazzi,* flashing their cameras in our faces as we made our way through. We were given preferential treatment at immigration, and I remember going through a kind of tunnel into an area where relatives of those released were waiting anxiously.

I was accosted by the BBC and Daily Telegraph journalists but brushed them all aside. I only wanted to see my June and Scott.

When we got through the crush, there was my June with my lovely niece Lyn who had driven up from Hythe to be with June when I arrived. It was a wonderful moment.

We had previously been given a pass to use the hotel facilities at the airport and where a room had been reserved for us.

Before going upstairs to our room, I remember briefly meeting this huge London fellow who had come with his mother to welcome his **brother** who had also been captured. This huge fellow whose name I cannot remember had a pint of beer in his hand and offered it to me. He was so happy for his brother, mother (and it seems everyone else), and he wanted me to share his joy by buying me a drink.

I had to refuse his kind offer and told him I would love to have a drink with him but unfortunately, "*I am allergic to anything containing alcohol.*"

He promptly asked if a lemonade and lime would be ok. I said *"wonderful"* and he went to the bar returning with a lemonade and lime. A lovely experience by a lovely human being who I had never seen before or since.

CHAPTER 8 - Back Home To Inverness

The following morning, June and I took the flight to Inverness Scotland, back to **Blarmore Avenue.**

It was good to see Scott and good to sleep in my own bed again with my dear June. We can never fully appreciate anything much until we are close to losing it. I had been deprived of a few things for a few months, and now I was able to see so vividly how important those things are to me.

I was quite underweight of course and was advised to seek medical attention. I did this and was also offered counselling which I politely declined. I did not feel threatened by my experiences in captivity. I put it all down to being in the wrong place at the wrong time.

And I still feel that way today. Life can throw things at us, but we all must deal with life on life's terms in the way we are able. I feel very grateful that I could come through the experience practically unscathed. I'm aware that some people do need extra attention when they have experienced high trauma, but perhaps I had it easy compared to some. Who knows?

I often say that AA has made me *better equipped* to deal with life on life's terms.

For the first couple of weeks, I did little more than enjoy my family, enjoy my AA meetings and appreciate how fortunate I was to be alive and relatively unharmed by my experiences.

During these first couple of weeks, I was visited by two members of MI6- the British Secret Intelligence Service. These two fellows pretended they were members of the British Army Intelligence Service, but during our discussions they inadvertently let a couple of things slip which made me realise just who their employers were.

They asked me many things about the facility I was held at, how the Mukhabarat behaved towards me, how the Iraqi Presidential Guard behaved when they interrogated me etc.

They were (I think), quite surprised when I told them I have no cross to bear and *no grudge against the Iraqi people*, that I believed I was simply a victim of circumstances that were set in motion long before the invasion. I told them our own previous and present governments had to share some of the blame for all that happened in not just Iraq but the middle East too.

One of them tried to get me to retract some of the things I was saying, but I told him just record it as I tell it. This is what I believe based upon my own experience in the middle east. I was clear that I thought it would be far better to continue talking to Saddam than bombing him.

I pointed out that the people who were doing what they were doing in Iraq was because they were instructed by their government to do it. They had no choice in the matter.

My aim was to put the whole issue into context and so *I asked both of these fellows if they had any choice but to come here to Inverness from London to ask me these questions.*

These two were not unpleasant people, just young men doing a job, but they left me alone after the second visit. I guess they thought I was a lost cause hahaha.

The only contact I had from them afterwards was on January 18th, 1991, I think it was when I was told over the phone that the place I had been held in Fallujah was now rubble, having been destroyed by the RAF.

I felt sick to the stomach wondering if Sloppy our dog and Ali who used to cook for us was still alive. I shall never know. I do remember being quite angry.

But now was the time to get on with my life. I had a little money in the bank, but this was entirely because of my June.

Although June had power of attorney from the time we were married, she did not use it to get access to my bank account whilst I was in captivity.

When I asked her why she didn't use some of the money in my account when it was freed up, she said she wanted to share the hardships I was going through and would have felt guilty if she had had a normal life whilst I was a hostage. Such is the quality of my June.

I have to say here that I know several men who were also locked up but did not have such caring wives waiting for them.

One guy had nothing left in his bank when he was released. His wife had withdrawn the lot and cleared off with someone else.

I had lost a lot of weight and had to get myself fit again. When I was ready, (after about 6/7 weeks), I went to the labour exchange to find work.

Land & Marine

The country was in "recession" and unemployment was about 9% of the workforce. They told me about a Job Centre scheme that was just starting where job seekers could use the facilities in an office in the town.

I applied to be accepted but they told me I was way down the waiting list. But I just kept pestering them, getting in their faces two or three times a day, until I think they just got fed up with me and made an opening for me.

I would go to this office every morning and use their fax machine to send off letters to companies. I had the use of a telephone and a typewriter and a copy machine. My letters were not chasing specific jobs but were speculative in nature with my blanket CV attached. I would make speculative phone calls to employers. Many would not even pick up the phone, but I kept on.

I was sending out up to 15-20 letters and faxes every day. I would apply for *any type of job* that I was able to do. I just wanted a job. It didn't matter what it was. Just a job. From project manager to deckhand, to steel fixer, to general labourer, it did not matter to me. **I just wanted a job.**

Within 8 days of starting my *job search* I found a job in the North Sea on a diving barge - (the Njord), owned and operated by *Land & Marine* – a subsidiary company of *Costain.*

It was amazing really. Here we were in a *"recession",* and I was offered a very good job over the phone.

My CV had gone to **Costain,** and they had passed it on to **Land & Marine**. It was a *'pier head jump"* meaning that I had to start right away.

When I accepted – (mid-afternoon) I was told that a hire car would be delivered to me the next morning.

Sure enough, at about 9am a rental car was delivered to our house at Blarmore Avenue. I checked it over and signed for it and took temporary ownership and responsibility for it.

An hour or so later I was on the road heading down to down to **Redcar** (where my mum came from originally) and joined the **Njord.** The journey of over 330 miles took me almost 9 hours including stops for food etc. I got to the site office around 6 o'clock in the evening. It was cold and dark and unfriendly, and I was tired.

I met the **project superintendent** who provided me with the terms of employment that was agreed over the phone the day before and gave me a copy signed by Costain. He then went on to explain to me my role in the operations.

My role was to be the **night master of the barge Njord** with a crew of 17 plus 22 commercial divers. This barge had an 8-point mooring system at the time but was later upgraded to a 12-point system.

The job entailed a pipe pull from one of the lay barges about 4,500m offshore.

We had to release the buoyancy tanks of the pipeline and allow the pipeline to settle in the pre-dredged trench on the seabed. It was a simple job really and we were well paid.

When I picked up my wage packet on the first week, I could not believe it. My gross pay before deductions was over £900 (pounds). This was early in 1991. With the sterling pound being what it is, this would equate to an economic value in 2020 of £2,123.52. *This for just one week's work.*

Of course, at that time, I was on emergency tax rate and took home less than 60% of that amount, but it was wonderful. The company were paying me each week and by the hour instead of a monthly salary like all other barge masters.

The weekly total became a ridiculous number of hours because they had a "loss of sleep allowance", "excessive hours allowance", "lodging allowance" and all kinds of other pay including 4 hours a day "travel". I was working 12 hours offshore – 7 days a week, but because of the terms of the contract and the fact that I was on hourly rates I was getting paid for about 22 – 24 hours a day. Anyway, the superintendent met me the morning after I had got my pay and told me there had been a mistake in the calculation. He said I should be on a monthly rate. He told me that the discrepancy would be adjusted over the coming weeks.

I desperately wanted the job, but I took a risky gamble. So, I told him as far as my contract went it was correct. He was really pissed that I wouldn't budge on it. I knew that the job had to continue, and I took a gamble that they could not find anyone else at such short notice.

Even though my pay was abnormally high, I knew that if the work stopped for just one hour it would cost the company more than a week's pay for me. These barges alone would cost the contractor in those times something like *35 thousand pounds a day* to hire as a bare barge. Then there was all the auxiliary stuff like tugs and safety vessels plus those other units indirectly connected to the project. If one-unit closes, even for a short time, it has a knock-on effect.

So, my gamble paid off, and I completed my contract (about 6 weeks) at the high rate of pay. It was brilliant. Even the superintendent was happy at the end of the contract as we had exceeded our targets.

About two weeks before the end of the contract, I had a call from *Gulf Dredging Co. in Kuwait*. They offered me a job. The country was now liberated, and the oil fires were in the process of being extinguished. I told them I was working right now but when my current contract ended, I would consider the offer.

A week later the personnel manager came to UK, and I met him in a place called *Carnforth* in the *Lake District*.

This was just across the *Pennines* from where I was based. We discussed terms and conditions. He offered me the same T&C as I was getting before which in truth was good.

But I refused and told him that I could not return on those T&C's particularly as my wife and son had suffered because of my *being held hostage* by the Iraqis. I suggested alternative terms and conditions to those he'd proposed. He said he was not authorised to give me what I was asking, and this would have to go before the Chairman and MD. Now I really and truly wanted the job, but I had to *"play the hand I was dealt"*.

I had long since learned that once you sign there is no use asking for more later. It just doesn't work that way with the Arabs. After about 3/4 more weeks of negotiating, we came to an agreement. On my return to Kuwait, I was to be appointed *Marine Supervisor* reporting directly to the *General Manager.*

Kuwait '91

The country was in a mess. Our marine equipment had been vandalized and one of our dredgers had been hit by explosive ordnance during the battles in Kuwait. It was badly damaged, but we set about repairing it.

The oil fires were still burning, and the skies were clearing as more and more of those fires were being extinguished. (Saddams men had set fire to over 600 oil wells on their retreat from Kuwait.)

One of my projects in October 1991 was the recovery of two large tugboats that had been sunk during the conflict. Both tugs were in critical navigable waters and were a hazard to navigating the channel into Shuwaikh Port, the primary port of Kuwait.

Each tug was laying in over 18 metres of water. My company hired a huge crane barge - (1,800 tonnes lifting capacity), and I lived onboard 24 hours a day for the duration of this project.

We successfully salvaged both and I was commended for my part in the operation, although to be fair, I was not the project manager, merely the company representative ensuring our salvage plan was being adhered to by the contractors who owned and operated the crane barge.

Our company was picking up many of the small to medium sized contracts being awarded by the government. But as usual, American companies were getting the lion's share of these contracts, and they were using their political strengths to accomplish this.

Unfortunately, the __British government was slow to act__ and lost tremendous opportunities to get in on the reconstruction of Kuwait.

GDC, being a Kuwaiti company was well placed to keep busy. My General Manager loaded one project after another into my lap. At one point in early 1992 I was managing 7 (seven) projects *simultaneously*.

Of course, this was only possible with the co-operation and support not only of my Chairman and GM but also of *the staff* I had under my care and control.

They performed magnificently, and it *was embarrassing for me to be given so much of the credit* when in truth these people, - (supervisors, engineers, surveyors, welders, boat crews, drivers, cooks, labourers, carpenters, etc. etc) were the ones doing the work. I was just overseeing and supporting them.

Prior to the invasion, we had begun the prestigious Amiri Diwan project. This entailed the construction of the new Seif Palace and the marina and harbour. The project value ran into hundreds of millions of dollars. We were awarded a large slice of the cake.

Our scope of work covered dredging and marine works. Unfortunately, much of our marine equipment had been sunk or damaged during the occupation and the subsequent liberation exercise.

Our flagship dredger, the *CSD Mubarak*, was damaged and while we searched for another similar dredger in the market that we could use instead, we could not get one until the following year. This would not be acceptable.

My chairman asked me to make an appraisal of how much it would cost to reinstate the CSD Mubarak, and the time frame to do this. I followed his instructions and submitted my report 4 days later.

After some negotiations with the main Contractor, the Consultant Engineers and the *Ministry of Interior Undersecretary*, our proposal to be allowed to make repairs to the CSD Mubarak and engage it for the bulk of the dredging works was accepted.

The American Consultant Engineers sent their inspectors daily whilst the restoration of the dredging equipment was taking place. I remember one of their inspectors saying to me that **"you will never have this ready in time"**.

He had a shock coming. Not only did we have it ready, but we also had it ready *before* the scheduled time.

In fairness to the guy, he did make a glowing report to the *Ministry of Interior* and the *Ministry of Public Works* on how well we had done to achieve our targets. This put us in a good light and was a bonus to us when we bid for other projects.

We had to recruit people from various countries and some of those were from Holland.

As the Dutch are reputed to be the *"Complete Masters"* of the dredging industry it was not always easy for me - a Brit, to deal with their often-arrogant attitude.

I don't think any of them had, throughout their careers, had to report to an Englishman on such a large project. It was a first for them and frankly almost to a man, they were not happy.

But after a while I gained their respect and we did in fact achieve a lot of very good results for our company. It was during this project that I was promoted to **Marine Superintendent**.

One interesting part of this project for me was the salvage of a sunken "A-Frame" Barge that was lying on the seabed in part of the channel that had been dredged prior to the invasion.

The barge was laying upside down with the A-Frame structure digging into the soft seabed.

At the time, we had contracted the use of a team of Brits to carry out U.O.D. (Unexploded Ordnance Demolition) operations, and I was able to get them to help me in the salvage of the barge. The team leader of the UOD group was an ex-Captain in the SBS (Special Boat Section) in the British military.

He was a decent fellow and being in the position he held he expected the salvage operation to be under his personal care and control.

However, I had already made a detailed plan of how to proceed and arranged a team meeting to go over the plans.

This is where we began to disagree on the modus operandi. I did not want the project to be delayed or affected as the plan I had put together relied upon three primary factors: COST, WEATHER CONDITIONS and TIDE CYCLES.

The ex-captain wanted to bring in a heavy lift crane barge which would impact all the primary factors.

As the discussions turned a bit confrontational during the early part of the meeting, I called a halt for a short break. During the break, I took the captain to one side and told him that although I wanted him and his team to be a part of the operation, there was just one leader - me. I went on to say that with or without his team the project would proceed as I already had a contingency for other EOD personnel to replace his team.

He told me face to face that he respected my directness and would now follow my plan without question.

The rest of the meeting went quite well, and the date was set to start the operations.

To cut a long story short, the whole project went like clockwork and from start to finish it took just 32 hours to salvage the barge.

After the salvage, the barge was sent to dry dock and in a further 3 weeks or so repairs and restoration to the barge was completed.

Our company expanded significantly during the following years and was split into various divisions:

Dredging, Shipbuilding, Planning, Civil Engineering, Construction, Equipment.

Masquerading As a Teacher

At some point in 1999, I left GDC and after taking several months holiday just doing nothing at all, I decided to embark on a new career.

I decided that as I had never been to university, it would be challenging to study for a degree in something that I could use to obtain employment in another field.

After investigating the opportunities available I discovered that the British Council College in Mansouria, Kuwait, held a very intense course which was accredited by Cambridge University in UK. The course was of *degree standard* and was reputed to be very intense. I decided to apply and sat the entrance exam. I passed and was accepted for the course.

I was 59 years old at the time of the course and yes, it was *very* intensive.

Except for myself and just one other person, all the remaining people on the course were already in the teaching profession and most of them - (possibly), found it easier than I did. All were at least 20-25 years younger than I was, mainly female.

We had several tutors and I found the going quite tough, but eventually I completed the course and was awarded my qualification.

I took up teaching for a while but really did not take to it. I enjoyed teaching the kids, but the some of the Kuwaiti adults were a pain in the arse to put it mildly.

I taught for **The British Council** plus **The British Institute for Training and Education**, amongst others and some private tuition from home.

We had now reached the era of the cell phone and most of the Kuwaitis aged over ten years of age had one. No problem in that except they would use them in the classroom if the tutor was not very capable of controlling them.

On one occasion, I was asked if I would teach a group of Kuwaiti **junior military officers** who were just so undisciplined the mind boggled. The tutor who had been assigned **gave it up in frustration** and it was offered to me.

Shortly after taking the class over, I soon realised why the other male teacher had given up on taking the class. He had been down that road before and he did not want a repeat performance. No sir.

These adult students were hard to handle and would walk over you if allowed them to do so.

But having dealt in the past with multi-national crews including Pathans from Afghanistan and northwest Pakistan, it would take more than these youngsters could put in my way to deter me.

And so, after seeing how they were behaving on the first day, I went back home that evening and made the following memo:

Gentlemen. It is my pleasure to be with you each day on this course to help you become proficient in the English Language. You are most welcome, but please allow me to make some things clear before we go on:

- *You are expected to arrive on time and always follow my instructions*
- *Late arrivals to MY classroom shall be sent home.*
- *The use of telephones in class is not allowed.*
- *Disruption to the learning process will not be tolerated.*

- *There are no compromises to these conditions, and your Commanding Officer shall be notified of any breach or failure to conform.*

Providing you are willing to abide by these conditions then you are welcome to stay. If you are not willing to do so then you are free to leave and find another tutor who is more suited to your personal needs.

Thank you for your co-operation................William Douglas.

The next morning, I placed a copy of the notice on the desk of each student.

After they were all seated, I asked the class if anyone had any comments.

Several protested saying things like I was treating them like children.

I reminded the class that they were *future military leaders* in Kuwait, and if they did not develop within themselves a strong ethic of behaviour, how could they expect others to obey their instructions and orders.

After a brief discussion amongst the class, it seemed that they were prepared to go along with my classroom etiquette.

I was asked by the *Principle of the College* why I had placed a bucket of water by my desk on which I had hung a small notice on the bucket which simply said; *"For nuisance cell phones".*

I told her it was a receptacle for any telephone that students had that rang more than once in the class. Not once was it ever used as such, but it did draw attention to the fact that cell phones in my classroom were not welcome, and this became somewhat of a talking point throughout the college.

The principle thought it was a bit over the top but let me do things my way. And it happened that at the end of the course, every single one of them received a pass of varying degree.

I also had the pleasure of tutoring (privately), the owner of a very large *General Trading Company* in Kuwait. This man was extremely well educated, and his spoken English was like something out of Eton College.

But all he wanted me to do was to coach him in the art of public speaking and wanted me to help with his presentations. He was very keen to learn and understand *the use of idioms* as he was often dealing with high profile Brits such as ministers, ambassadors etc.

He was of the mind that by introducing a few idioms into his presentation speeches would enhance his connection with the target audience.

He was a really nice gentleman, and we got along extremely well. He would invite me to his lovely home on occasion and introduced me to some very influential people who were helpful in the following years.

The Canada Experience

In July 2000, June and I went off to Waterloo, Ontario, in Canada. We went to visit a friend of mine (Jean) in the fellowship of AA.

I first met Jean in 1989 when she was visiting Kuwait with her husband Archie. He was a professor at the *University of Waterloo Ontario* and was spending a few months in Kuwait lecturing at Kuwait University.

After they left in 1990, Jean and I stayed in touch by email. Sometime during our correspondence in 1999, Jean mentioned that she was going to the AA World Convention the following year

On 1st July. 40 of us, (all members of AA and Al-Anon), set out on a coach journey that was to take us to Minneapolis to attend the *AA World Convention.*

Even the bus drivers were in AA. It was a magic trip, and we stopped off overnight at a hotel in *Chicago* before arriving in *Minneapolis*.

After having an amazing experience at the convention, we returned to Waterloo arriving around 8th July 2000.

Without going into a long story, I purchased a house for us in Waterloo. It was a lovely place and June was delighted.

Later in the month, we returned to Scotland, and before I went back to Kuwait, we visited the company who had been storing our furniture for the previous 7 years. The name of the company was WHITES, but it has a BLACK reputation for evermore after our visit to their premises.

We had paid this company an average of £1,000.00 every year and we had been assured that it was all stored in an air-conditioned warehouse in self-contained enclosed cubicles.

The reality was that we found our entire household belongings kept behind curtains in a *dreary loft* in a building in the town of Forres in Morayshire. There was dust everywhere and some of our stuff had visible damage.

It was disgraceful and we were shocked as we had been paying out year after year in the belief that this company was good for their word. The local manager was way out of his depth and kept making excuse after excuse.

And so, I contacted the *MD* of the company who was based in *Southampton,* and after much argument and threats from me to sue the company for fraudulent behaviour, the company agreed to pack and dispatch the entire contents to our new home in Canada free of charge.

June returned to Canada and was able to receive the freight at our new home. It was hard for her, but she managed to set everything up in her usual caring way.

I travelled from Kuwait arriving in Canada on 30th November 2000.

We had a plan that I would pack everything up in Kuwait and send it to Canada and we would reside in Canada after I found work. The plan was for me to take up a teaching position at the university.

But I have learned in the past that plans sometimes change. This plan was no exception.

At first the novelty of the seasonal snow was okay, but after three weeks of heavy snowfalls and extreme cold, I told June I could imagine living and working here. I would return to Kuwait and visit here periodically instead.

This concept was not received at all favourably by my June.

Eventually, after I admitted having made a colossal error of judgement by not thinking it all through carefully before purchasing the property, we sold the house and everything in it and left Canada in 2001.

June came back to Kuwait, and we stayed there until 2017.

Loss Adjusting

In 2001, I had had enough of teaching and decided there was an opportunity for me to enter the realms of *Loss Adjusting* on Marine Insurance Claims.

My marine background helped and taking some written exams and several interviews, I was accepted by the *International Institute of Marine Surveyors* and awarded a licence to practice as a *Loss Adjuster*.

I quite enjoyed most of this work but not all of it. Sometimes there would be claims by the insured to investigate where we had to check damaged items against those that were undamaged and yet lodged together in the claim.

This could be very tedious work and for me totally uninteresting. But on the other hand, a *tricky marine claim* could be very absorbing and interesting. We just took the jobs that were offered and were paid according to our fee scales.

I remember particularly one project I was given to investigate: It entailed storm damage which had resulted in heavy losses to a contractor undertaking a Dredging and Marine Construction project in Fintas - Kuwait.

After quite intensive investigation into the claim, I was able to recommend to the insurers *(Kuwait Insurance Company)*, that the entire claim be declared null and void. The basis of my decision centred around a clear breach of contract relating to the required precautionary measures required by the contractor.

The contractor had tried to save a considerable amount of money by reducing the required height of the temporary shore protection as demanded by the insurance policy and the contract.

I discovered that the datums they had used to determine the height of the temporary shore protection, were 47 centimetres lower that the contractual and insurance policy requirements.

They had used a Kudams' datum instead of a K.L.C.D. - (Kuwait Land Chart Datum), ant this had been *overlooked by the consultant engineers.*

It was because of my local knowledge of these datums and the related benchmarks that I was able to conduct my own survey and prove that the breach of contract had occurred.

The claim from the contractor amounted to about $1,750,000.00 and because of my report, the Insurance company was not liable to pay out anything.

When the Insurance company sent the contractor a preliminary assessment, there was uproar. The contractor called in their Contracts Director from Saudi Arabia and all parties agreed to use an arbitrator who was brought in from USA.

A heated meeting took place, and I was there to support the argument I had submitted to the Kuwait Insurance Company.

At the end of the meeting, I asked the arbitrator how he would report his findings.

Off the record, he told me that the contractor had no claim, and he would report this to the client who was in fact *The Ministry of Defence.*

But being Kuwait, where corruption is the order of the day, there was some negotiating done behind closed doors and eventually the *Kuwait Insurance Company* agreed to pay the contractor 35% of their claim in order to maintain good relations.

When I was told of this by the manager in the local office of KIC I went slightly "nuclear". It transpired that the contractor had on the board of its directors, two members who were also on the board of Insurance Company. And so, over coffee and dates in the Diwaniya, the deal was done to pay out $610,000.00 of the original claim instead of $0.00 as I had recommended and indeed proven the case.

I was quite disgusted with the Insurance Company and as such declined all and any future work from them.

Of course, this was a bit like shooting myself in the foot as KIS were and still are the biggest Insurance Company in Kuwait and they gave me a fair amount of work. But principles are principles and they had crossed a line with me.

During this period of loss adjusting, I learned a lot. I discovered that the real reason we have Loss Adjusters is because so many of the claims received are quite phony and fraudulent.

An example of this was a claim by another big contractor who was engaged in a multi-million-dollar project to install storm drains in a residential area.

The contractor lodged a claim for damages on the project itself, and they had every right to do this under the terms of the policy.

When I received the claim documents and went through them, it appeared to me that everything was above board. The claim was based upon Storm Damage during a freak period of torrential rain. This had resulted in the ingress of sand into the newly constructed system of culverts.

The theme of the project was a system of culverts that were engineered and installed using huge micro-tunnelling machines.

This created a system below the existing ground level.

These culverts were huge, about 3mx 3m square and accessed by various manholes in a dozen or so places throughout the system.

I toured the (overground) site with the project manager employed by the contractor and noted that when the observer considered the condition below by considering these manholes from ground level, it gave the impression that this was the condition throughout the whole warren of culverts.

But then I had an instinctive thought that I should go below ground myself and check out the culverts.

I requested the project manager to make available to me a crane with a personnel basket to be placed at my disposal. When I told him why, he was reluctant to help making one excuse after another, - (equipment not available at this time etc. etc.).

Not to be deterred, I hired a 7-metre ladder and with the help of a couple of others I went underground using the access manholes. And what a revelation it was.

Indeed, what the contractor had done, was to gather materials including sand, and place this material in heaps at the bottom of every manhole. By doing so, it was revealed that the volume of debris and materials the contractor was claiming for was in fact a small percentage of the claimed quantity.

I spent the rest of the day touring this underground warren of tunnels which was about 4.5 metres below existing ground level. The following day I did the same.

What the contractor had done, was to gather materials including sand, and place this in heaps at the bottom of every manhole.

When I had finished, the project manager was obviously embarrassed by my findings and was implying that his supervisors were responsible for the deception and would be punished.

I knew he was lying because during my underground inspections I cam across a small Bobcat loader in the culvert that had been used to gather the offending materials and heap them below the manholes.

But I did not want to involve myself with the internal affairs of the contractor and so allowed him to bethink I accepted his accusation that he had no knowledge of what had happened.

My brief was to assess the situation and report my findings to the Insurance Company. This is what I got paid for.

Ultimately, after further discussions between the insured and the insurers, the claim was reduced to about 10% of the original, although my own assessment was approximately half of that (about 5.5%).

Such is the business of Loss Adjustment on Insurance Claims.

Embassy Warden

In 2001, I was approached by a member of the British Embassy in Kuwait who asked me if I would like to become a warden for them.

This entailed being a go-between and liaison person for members of the British Community in and around the area of Kuwait in which I lived.

There were over six hundred British expats in my area and after giving it some consideration, I agreed to do it. I was entrusted with a variety of information and details of persons in the community and had direct access to the Consul and the Ambssador.

It probably sounds more sophisticated than it was, but it basically provided a service to the community and helped the FCO to prepare plans in case of emergencies such as happened in 1990. We had monthly meetings at the Embassy of wardens and ambassadorial staff and there was always plenty of booze handed around.

I was considered a bit odd being a British Expatriate who did not drink alcohol *(especially when it was free)*, but after mentioning my allergy to alcohol it was rarely pushed at me to *"have just one"*.

Then in 2002 when it became clear that the **Bush & Blair** administrations were going to invade Iraq, I was very opposed to it *and voiced my serious concerns* to both my fellow citizens and to the Ambassador.

Unfortunately, I rarely found, (if indeed I ever did), anyone who shared my concerns.

The jingoism that was being pushed into the media by the likes of CNN, BBC, Fox News, and so many other Western media outlets was horrendous to me. And most people were being convinced by this nonsense.

That Saddam Hussein had developed a credible nuclear weapon since his defeat in 1990 was totally impossible.

In the inevitable discussions, I took pains to show that since 1991, Iraq had been overflown EVERY SINGLE DAY by US and British warplanes.

Anything on Iraqi territory *looking suspiciously threatening* was destroyed by bombs or missiles. It was impossible for them to develop anything near the point of being a threat to its neighbours or the Western countries. *Absolute tosh.*

Even most of the Kuwaitis that I knew were in favour of invading Iraq and getting rid of Saddam. It was nothing to do with a threat. It was all to do with control of the whole Middle East by the USA and Israel.

But this sort of commentary from myself and some British politician activists like Wedgewood Benn, George Galloway and many others were met with disdain, even to the point of being accused of being unpatriotic.

But I continued to voice my fears that invasion of Iraq would have huge repercussions. It proved to be the case as recent history has demonstrated. (ISIS being just one disastrous by-product of the invasion). And so, in my frustration I kept writing to the media to express my opposition. *And guess what?*

One day, a letter I wrote to the Arab Times was published on the front page. It was an *open letter to Bush and Blair.* I was surprised it was published but there it was. The date was Tuesday 11th March 2002

Ironically, there was a Wardens Meeting at the embassy that evening, and I phoned to let them know I would be late. My friend Ed F. had come in from London, and we were having dinner together.

When I eventually arrived at the Embassy all the wardens and others were engaged in general chit chat. It seems the business meeting had finished and now was the time for *"networking"*.

Not a single person of those present mentioned to me, the article in the *Arab Times* and yet it was the paper that 90% of English-speaking expats read daily.

Obviously, this had been discussed prior to my arrival, and I felt a little uncomfortable and felt I was being somewhat ostracised.

And then the bombshell came.

The Ambassador of the day, *Ambassador Muir*, approached me as I was chatting to one of the other wardens. He did not offer his hand as is customary but instead waver a copy of the days Arab Times in front of me.

He just said this: "Mr. Douglas, this is not the kind of thing that helps our government at all, especially coming from a warden of this embassy."

I just gave him my best look of disgust and replied: *"No ambassador, this kind of letter to our prime minister should never happen if our diplomatic corps did their job".*

He was furious and stormed off. We never spoke again, and he was later replaced by *Ambassador Wilton* with whom I got on with quite well.

The absolute irony of all this was that this same ambassador later became one of no less than fifty ex-ambassadors' appealing by a letter Prime Minister Blair condemning the invasion of Iraq that took place in March 2003.

My Letter to Bush and Blair

Here is the letter that I sent to the Arab Times and referred to above:

Open Letter to President George W. Bush and Prime Minister Blair

Dear George and Tony

When the American and British governments acted after the events that shook the world on 11th September 2001, most people I know were supportive.

Now, just a few months later, those very same people are having serious doubts about a lot of things. One thing I keep hearing is "double standards". I don't need to go into detail about what those "double standards" are.

Gentlemen, before you set yourselves up as the guardian of my standards, I suggest you get some of your own. And, when you speak virtuously about putting things in order, please ensure that your own houses are in order before you start on the rest of us.

Your collective arrogance is frightening and entirely unacceptable to myself and many other decent law-abiding people of this world.

I remind you both that YOU are very privileged people in as much as when and where you were born, raised, and educated. Most people on our planet and even in British and American society do not get such a good start in life. But I do not hold this against you. I just like to put things in perspective.

And today, you have both risen to attain positions of tremendous power. With is power comes huge responsibility to those you have sworn to serve. Yes, and I repeat, to serve.

You now are positioned and equipped to either create better things for society or perpetuate the bad stuff. YES.............You really do have choices.

But now, your recent behaviour and actions on the world stage is leading many of us - (and I include myself here), into thinking that you are equally, if not more dangerous than the terrorists we are now trying to bring to justice.

You appear to condone the State Terrorism that Israel is conducting under the ego-maniac Ariel Sharon, whilst at the same time, condemning State Terrorism by the Iranian regime. Sharon's soldiers are even killing ambulance men of the Red Cross who are trying to tend to the injured and suffering casualties of the Israeli aggression on civilians in Gaza. And neither of you are opposing this action.

You are even justifying the perceived use of nuclear weapons whenever this may git your agenda. You have named Russia as one of the countries that you might have to use these terrible weapons against. Are the Russians not your friends these days or are you deliberately trying to revive and impose a "cold war" environment on our planet. My father told me that politics was "a dirty business," but this really takes the cake.

Who would have friends that openly announce that if push comes to shove, they will nuke their own friends? Where are your values, your standards, your ethics? What kind of diplomacy is this?

People who were supporting you just a few weeks, months back are now SPEAKING out against you. How much longer before they are going to ACT against you?

I now put to you two powerful leaders this question. When will the NEXT "nine-eleven" incident take place?

I ask this because, the way you two are behaving it is inevitable that your policies and reckless and unjust actions will lead to more resistance and accelerate the occurrence of such an event.

The people of the world want to see fair play. We do not see it right now. Please address this problem before it's too late. It is your power to do so.

William Douglas ....10th March 2002

Ambassador's Letter to Blair

Ironically, in early 2004 and after the illegal invasion of Iraq began, former British Ambassadors signed an open letter to Blair. Here is the letter sent by more than 50 former British ambassadors to Tony Blair, urging him either to influence US policy in the Middle East or to stop backing it:

" *We the undersigned former British ambassadors, high commissioners, governors and senior international officials, including some who have long experience of the Middle East and others whose experience is elsewhere, have watched with deepening concern the policies which you have followed on the Arab-Israel problem <u>and Iraq</u>, in close co-operation with the United States.*

Following the press conference in Washington at which you and President Bush restated these policies, we feel the time has come to make our anxieties public, in the hope that they will be addressed in Parliament and will lead to a fundamental reassessment.

The decision by the USA, the EU, Russia and the UN to launch a Road Map for the settlement of the Israel/Palestine conflict raised hopes that the major powers would at last make a determined and collective effort to resolve a problem which, more than any other, has for decades poisoned relations between the West and the Islamic and Arab worlds.

The legal and political principles on which such a settlement would be based were well established: President Clinton had grappled with the problem during his presidency; the ingredients needed for a settlement were well understood and informal agreements on several of them had already been achieved. But the hopes were ill-founded.

Nothing effective has been done either to move the negotiations forward or to curb the violence.

Britain and the other sponsors of the Road Map merely waited on American leadership but waited in vain.

Worse was to come. After all those wasted months, the international community has now been confronted with the announcement by Ariel Sharon and President Bush of new policies which are one-sided and illegal, and which will cost yet more Israeli and Palestinian blood.

Our dismay at this backward step is heightened by the fact that you yourself seem to have endorsed it, abandoning the principles which for nearly four decades have guided international efforts to restore peace in the Holy Land and which have been the basis for such successes as those efforts have produced.

This abandonment of principle comes at a time when rightly or wrongly we are portrayed throughout the Arab and Muslim world as partners in an illegal and brutal occupation in Iraq.

The conduct of the war in Iraq has made it clear that there was no effective plan for the post-Saddam settlement.

All those with experience of the area predicted that the occupation of Iraq by the Coalition forces would meet serious and stubborn resistance, as has proved to be the case.

To describe the resistance as led by terrorists, fanatics and foreigners is neither convincing nor helpful.

Policy must take account of the nature and history of Iraq, the most complex country in the region.

However much Iraqis may yearn for a democratic society, the belief that one could now be created by the Coalition is naive.

This is the view of virtually all independent specialists in the region, both in Britain and in America.

We are glad to note that you and the president have welcomed the proposals outlined by Lakhdar Brahimi.

We must be ready to provide what support he requests, and to give authority to the United Nations to work with the Iraqis themselves, including those who are now actively resisting the occupation, to clear up the mess.

The military actions of the Coalition forces must be guided by political objectives and by the requirements of the Iraq theatre itself, not by criteria remote from them.

It is not good enough to say that the use of force is a matter for local commanders.

Heavy weapons unsuited to the task in hand, inflammatory language, the current confrontations in Najaf and Falluja, all these have built up rather than isolated the opposition.

The Iraqis killed by coalition forces probably total between 10,000 and 15,000 (it is a disgrace that the coalition forces themselves appear to have no estimate), and the number killed in the last month in Falluja alone is apparently several hundred, including many civilians, men, women and children.

Phrases such as `We mourn each loss of life. We salute them, and their families for their bravery and their sacrifice,' apparently referring only to *those who have died on the Coalition side, are not well judged to moderate the passions those killings arouse.*

We share your view that the British Government has an interest in working as closely as possible with the United States on both these related issues, and in exerting real influence as a loyal ally.

We believe that the need for such influence is now a matter of the highest urgency.

If that is unacceptable or unwelcome there is no case for supporting policies which are doomed to failure.

Signatories: Brian Barder; Paul Bergne; John Birch; David Blatherwick; Graham Boyce; Julian Bullard; Juliet Campbell; Bryan Cartledge; Terence Clark; David Colvin; Francis Cornish; James Craig; Brian Crowe; Basil Eastwood; Stephen Egerton; William Fullerton; Dick Fyjis-Walker; Marrick Goulding; John Graham; Andrew Green; Vic Henderson; Peter Hinchcliffe; Brian Hitch; Archie Lamb and David Logan.

Christopher Long; Ivor Lucas; Ian McCluney; Maureen MacGlashan; Philip McLean; Christopher MacRae; Oliver Miles; Martin Morland; Keith Morris; Richard Muir; Alan Munro; Stephen Nash; Robin O'Neill; Andrew Palmer; Bill Quantrill; David Ratford; Tom Richardson; Andrew Stuart; David Tatham; Crispin Tickell; Derek Tonkin; Charles Treadwell; Hugh Tunnell; Jeremy

You can see that despite the way that *Ambassador Muir* condemned me in front of others at the Embassy almost 2 years previously, he did sign the letter above as can be seen.

But despite everything, including the condemnation by the UN, the unlawful invasion of Iraq began on 17th March 2003. And the disastrous results of that invasion are still being felt throughout the whole world.

Unjust action and inactions too have created monster after monster over the succeeding years including the so-called Islamic State (ISIS) and other terrorist factions worldwide.

Will we EVER learn?

Evacuation Of Kuwait

As the build up to go to war was being orchestrated by the efforts of the Bush/Blair alliance, the media were getting in on the act, and it became the main news item in most of the western press.

I was still ineffectually protesting and even the British public went out on the streets of London, Manchester, Glasgow and other major cities of UK. Over one million people hit the streets but to no avail.

Blair overruled the UK parliament and the unlawful assault on Iraq began on 17 March 2003.

The FCO were *"advising"* the Brits to be ready to leave Kuwait before the hostilities break out. My June like most others, became convinced by the rhetoric from our embassy and the FCO.

And so, inevitably, a mass evacuation of British and American and other western expatriates began in February 2003.

June went to Scotland and stayed with our friends Christine and Don, in the hope that she would soon return to Kuwait. But it happened that her return was delayed for some time and she was offered rental of a house in Raigmore Estate which she took over the tenancy in April 2003.

I was totally unconvinced by the stories of Scud missiles, chemical and nuclear weapons etc. and of course I refused to be repatriated to UK.

My friend and work colleague Bill L. also stayed as he was of the same mind as I was and knew it was just *scaremongering* to support the politicians.

Hundreds of thousands of Kuwaitis also left the country and it was easy to get around as there was much less traffic. So, it had its benefits for those of us who remained in Kuwait.

As we got close to the time of the invasion the country abounded with news reporters from far and wide.

One day, just about two or three days prior to 17th March, Bill and I were approached by a television crew from BBC.

We were asked to voice our views as Brits who had stayed on.

Of course, I went into my usual condemnation of our government of the day and mentioned that there could not possibly be nuclear weaponry available to Iraqi forces.

I even asked if the interviewer, a woman, would be here right now if she believed that Iraq possessed nuclear weapons. She did not answer.

We were told our interviews would be aired on the 6 o'clock news that evening in UK. But it was apparently deemed inappropriate as I was told later by the same person who interviewed us. Her name was Kate who was quite popular on BBC television news.

On 17th March, the sirens went off all over Kuwait indicating that we were at war with Iraq. This racket went on several times a day when the occasional SCUD missile would penetrate Kuwait territory.

But to my knowledge very few SCUDS were fired into Kuwait territory and on one occasion it was claimed that a scud had hit the fishing jetty that my old company had installed close to the Souk at Dasman.

On the other hand, Iraq was devastated by the bombing by the Americans and Brits. The infrastructure was almost destroyed. Power stations, bridges, ministry buildings, all of it was demolished.

As a result of all this devastation, law and order quickly broke down all over the country.

Looting became the norm and total chaos ensued.

This was the outcome that the father of George Bush predicted in 1991 when he stopped the invasion of Iraq that the hawks wanted.

He, (George Bush senior) had the wisdom to take the advice of his generals on the ground. Schwarzkopf foresaw what could happen and he did not want to see his army engaged in combat inside Iraq for years to come.

But now, some 12 years later, it was his son George W. Bush who was at the helm and with the warmongering people he had surrounded himself with there was no stopping them.

He had appointed as his Defence Secretary a man called Donald Rumsfeld, who was a hawk. Then he had Dick Cheyney as his Vice President. There was Paul

Wolfwitz, Condoleezza Rice, John Bolton and many other hawkish people in his entourage. No wonder it developed into the critical path it has followed since then.

Bush claimed the war was over, (in fact, as we predicted, it had just begun) and the infamous victory claim was made by George W. Bush on the deck on the aircraft carrier USS Abraham Lincoln on May 1, 2003, was a theatrical farce and of course a complete falsehood.

After The Fiasco

Because of the extent of the devastation of Iraq, the Americans dominated the selection process of which companies would get the reconstruction work.

The idea was that the pre-qualification documents that prospective companies would need to comply with for any tenders were geared almost exclusively to American companies.

The big boys like Schlumberger, Brown & Root, Halliwell, Kellog, Bechtel, Fluor, etc were all heavily represented at the several meetings I attended when these tenders were being offered.

Brown & Root seemed to get the lion's share of the major civil-engineering projects whilst Schlumberger and Fluor were getting the main contracts to repair and upgrade the oil sector works.

The British and French companies were almost side-lined but did manage to get some of the smaller projects.

As I pointed out previously, the conditions presented in the documents were so geared towards the US companies that others were unable to comply with many of the technical conditions.

Most of the contracts had two main elements.

1. The Technical Bid

2. The Commercial Bid

This meant that if the technical bid did not comply in its entirety, the commercial bid would not even be opened.

Everything was above board legally, but because these huge US companies had such enormous capital and resources, these huge resources were a prime element when drawing up the bid docs.

And so, for example if a UK company was very capable of doing the work asked for in a particular contract and put in a technical bid, it may not have been able to comply with the terms and conditions and so would not have a chance of submitting a commercial bid because of this.

It could be for example that the company had to show where they had completed a let's say one-billion-dollar contract in the last three years. The company had never had a one-billion-dollar contract in its entire history, but its otherwise technical ability was more than adequate.

But the one billion conditions could not be met and shown in the technical bid and so everything stopped there.

The huge US companies on the other hand could show that they could comply with the one billion condition and so they were able then to submit their own Commercial Bid.

Naturally, they had the monopoly and so they were getting greatly overpriced contracts which the interim Iraqi government would pay from the oil reserves either in oil or in dollars. Whatever way it was done, it was all a win-win situation if you represented a huge US company.

During this time, the Kuwaiti husband of my close friends made me an offer to get involved with some dredging works in Umm Qasr port in Southern Iraq. He had the contacts and explained all I had to do was make a bid for the works *through one of his own companies.*

The main contract had already been awarded to Brown & Root and his company and because dredging was my game, he wanted someone he could trust to oversee the whole project as a project director. He told me I could personally *earn* as much as one million dollars in less than 12 months.

I was very tempted but at the same time I was disgusted at the way the Iraqis were being systematically exploited. And so, after giving it some thought I declined to take part.

Consequently, the husband of my friend, who had assumed I would come onboard with this venture, was upset with me and HE lost the opportunity to make himself several millions as he had to involve another party that wanted a much bigger share of the funds that would have been coming to me.

Anyway, another opportunity came along with a large company in Kuwait. This was a company involved in many projects in the region. The name was *Mushrif.*

Mushrif

Mushrif Trading & Contracting Co, KSCP had a turnover of many millions, and their operations covered various fields of activity including:

- Civils and Infrastructure
- Oil and Gas
- Treatment Plants
- Pumping Stations
- Facilities O&M

After a meeting with the owner representative, I agreed to help the company set up a new division They had a strong desire to enter the *Dredging & Marine Construction* field of operations.

They wanted me to sign a contract of employment with the company and made me a very good offer. I declined to join the group but agreed to act as *Marine Consultant* on a freelance basis. It turned out to be the right decision.

And so, I went away from the meeting promising to prepare an outline business plan to set up a *Marine Division* as was the desire of the owner.

When I had done this, I set up a meeting with his board of directors and showed them the presentation of the plan, the budget, the time frame, etc.

I was not sure of the outcome because I had not glamorized the proposal. My job was not to sell anything but to present the *"money owners"* with the bare bones of setting up a division and the also the hard facts.

Sure, there was huge profits in the *Marine Construction & Dredging Industry,* but there were huge losses too. I illustrated all of this with figures and examples for actual projects I had been involved in.

Anyway, the company decided to set up a division and my involvement as consultant was desired.

I was sent hither and yonder to procure marine equipment and personnel. I went to *India* to recruit manpower, to *Singapore* to purchase barges and tugs, to *Dubai* to purchase a dredger, to *UK* to purchase a survey vessel and to interview a couple of hydrographic surveyors.

Again, to *UK* to purchase some Piling Equipment from Dawson Piling. *Robin Dawson,* the owner of Dawson Piling Company was an old pal of mine and he gave us a good deal on several items of equipment

I went to *Holland* to purchase some specialized underwater pumps and after about 11 months we were up and ready to go. All in all, I procured on behalf of the company around $11.75 million of equipment- just to start things off.

In the meantime, the company had bid for their first Marine Construction Project which was the *Marine Science Centre* at Fintas. This project began in 2004 and *Mushrif* put in a bid of just over $40 million dollars. ($40,130,700.00)

The client was *Kuwait University* and Mushrif was the lowest bidder. The next lowest was almost 10 million dollars more - 49.8 million dollars.

A bad sign, but the owners were determined to make inroads and wanted THIS project even if they lost money on it. And they did lose money for more reasons than one.

The owners believed in employing Brits for senior positions in the company. Nothing wrong with that, if you source the RIGHT people. But the company instead was employing some real *"cowboys".*

For a smart businessman, the MD had a real blind spot. If a smooth-talking Brit was granted an interview for a senior position and had a seemingly good track record, the company would employ him.

But although *some* of these Brits were very good, there were those that were very bad too. And this cost Mushrif a lot. And I mean A LOT.

For example, he employed as Operations Manager on the project a guy named *Alan H.*

Alan had an impressive CV and was able to handle people of all disciplines. No doubt about that. But Alan had a major defect. *He was bone idle.* He never followed up on things that were critical to the success of the project.

He should have anticipated that owing to the sub strata in some places throughout the project being quite different to the results shown in a correlation exercise using bore log data provided by the client, this huge difference would result in the sheet pile quantities allocated for the project were far short of what was required.

The sheet piles, *being a long lead item* that came from *UK and Germany,* were the significant cause of delays. These delays were not confined to a single item of operation but had a *knock-on effect* on other activities too.

The result was project overrun and liquidated damages were imposed by the client.

Coupled with the very low bid price Mushrif lost a packet on this, - their very first venture into Marine works.

I could see how this was going to end long before the sheet piles episode that I give here as just one example.

I warned the owners *many times* on the pitfalls I could see, but he did not act upon my advice. In the end, long before the project really got under way, I let go of the company. I was in danger of losing my reputation. I was not going to let that happen.

The owners pleaded with me to hang on, but I told the MD point blank.

"What is the point? You employed my services to advise you, but when I do give you solid advice you are just smiling and agreeing but you take no action. Sooner or later, this will come back to bite you on the bum."

I did help him out on a couple of occasions after that, but he was digging himself deeper into the holes with some of those he'd employed. It was sad to watch from afar, but it was his money – his monkeys – not mine.

I recall one evening when I had a call from his *operations Manager* telling me that one of the rock barges had broken free of its moorings and was being dashed onto the shore by heavy seas.

Although I had finished my involvement with that company, my curiosity led me to go down to see what had transpired.

When I arrived at around midnight at the scene of the incident, the MD was there with other members of his marine department personnel. He was obviously a bit embarrassed at me seeing the mess, but I took him aside and suggested a solution.

Anyway, after implementing my rescue plan, the barge was back afloat in about 36 hours and after an underwater inspection of the hull was carried out, everyone was relieved that there was no significant damage to the barge.

It was another sad lesson for **Mushrif,** and it was causing the company to lose more than just money. Their reputation with the client and indeed other potential clients was being eroded by the day.

It was inevitable that this project was doomed to overrun the schedule, and I believe that by the time the project was completed, it had cost *Mushrif* several hundred thousand dollars in **liquidated damages** apart from the huge project overspend facing *Mushrif.*

This project saw the beginning of the end to the *Marine Division* activities of *Mushrif* and within a year of the project completion he was winding up the division.

Dredging Consultant

Soon after this, I was approached by GDC to ask me if I would be interested in working for them again. I was not keen on working full time for them but agreed to consult on a fee basis.

The work involved the managing of operations of a trailer suction dredger that they had recently acquired. This dredger was named *Danet Al Shuaiba.*

I was told that the operation of the equipment was not producing the results they had expected.

They had brought in a very experienced person from The Great Lakes Dredging Company and despite his best efforts, the performance of the operations was not satisfactory.

It was thought that with my own experience on Trailer Suction Dredgers and previous experience on how the company operated, the dredging methods could be improved.

After we came to a suitable agreement, I was given a free reign to implement whatever means necessary to get the work on track.

The vessel was manned by deck and catering crews from Philippines and by engine room staff from Sri Lanka.

The project the vessel was working on was a sediment cleaning project. It entailed removing sedimentary deposits from the seabed of Shuwaikh Port and the 8 km long approach channel into the port. The project value was around $10.45 million dollars.

My first step was to get the dredging department manager to introduce me to the crew whilst the vessel was operating. The work carried on 24/7 non-stop, except for repairs of refuelling etc.

After the manager explained the purpose of my involvement, I arranged with the Master of the vessel to allow me to visit daily to monitor operational technique.

The Master was a guy who **ruled the ship with an iron hand**. The crew were obviously fearful of him which to me was very apparent. I'm all for discipline on marine equipment but this was not just discipline – **it was fear.**

Anyway, without boring you with details, in a matter of about 10 days of operations I had a very clear understanding of things.

I discovered, that unbeknown to the owners - (GDC), four of the deck crew were brothers of the Master of the vessel.

Under his orders, these brothers were bullying and beating anyone, and I mean ANYONE who did not toe a line that the Master had demanded.

This meant that they were being cheated of overtime pay, food rations, and other benefits that the company was **paying in cash** to the master for distribution.

He would get the crew to sign for money ***they were not actually receiving*** and was not supplying the quantity of food and supplies he claimed to be getting from the ship's chandlers.

And so, I altered the way things were being done.

I arranged that all cash payments to the Master were halted and overtime was paid directly into the seamen's accounts instead.

The food now came from the chandler, but payment was by approved invoice.

So petty cash to the Master was now stopped in every direction which had the effect of taking just some of his abusive power away.

The Master was furious with me and did everything he could to make things difficult for me. But I had faced far worse than this guy in my career and he did not scare me a bit.

To cut a long story short, through our HR department we sourced another mixed nationality deck crew.

When I had interviewed and selected a new deck crew and everything was now in place, I fired all the deck crew, including one guy who had helped me uncover all the crookeries. I fired this guy to protect him from repercussions in his home country from the Master and his brothers.***(We re-employed him about 6 months later and sent him an air ticket.)***

After all this, we made a load of changes in how the operations were carried out and we became profitable at last.

I consulted with GDC in this way for about 6 months in total and they were pleased with the outcome and so was I.

I suggested to them that in future they avoid recruiting from single sources as I have found that this can easily lead to cronyism and corruption. I've seen it time and again in my career.

Mixing apples and oranges may not work but mixing nationalities on marine vessels does...............most of the time anyhow.

CHAPTER 9 - Dredging Division Manager.

The company fired the Dredging Manager they had previously employed and offered me the position of Dredging Division Manager.

The company was growing again, and the prospects were looking bright.

And so, I now re-joined the company on a full-time basis. I negotiated a good deal and was provided with a few nice perks.

I reported initially to the new chairman Mr. Manaf Al Hanna. I got on very well with him and he was always inviting me to his office to advise him and certain matters relating to our dredging division.

He had no dredging experience whatsoever but was often willing – (up to a point), to take onboard suggestions for improvements to our company.

It was because of one of our discussions that I convinced him to purchase for my division a jack-up-barge.

He asked me to source one and I did so. We purchased a new jack-up-barge from a broker I knew, and it soon became a useful asset to us.

Sometime during this period, we came to know that Mushrif Trading & Contracting Co were breaking up their Marine Division and selling their assets.

Amongst these assets were the survey vessel I had purchased on their behalf in UK; a tugboat I had purchased for them in Malaysia and a couple of rock barges I had also purchased for them in Singapore.

And now, ironically, I was negotiating for GDC with MUSHRIF to acquire these assets.

Although we had MUSHRIF over a barrel I was adamant that we offered a fair price. I pointed out that MUSHRIF had previously on purchase covered ALL the import duties and licencing costs which were a substantial savings to us.

Anyway, after negotiations were finished, we became the new owners.

These included:

- ➢ Rock barge of 6,000 dwt.

- ➢ Rock barge of 3,000 dwt.

- ➢ Tugboat of 3,200 bhp.

- ➢ Survey Vessel with all survey equipment

- ➢ Work barge fitted with spuds.

We now had over 40 marine vessels in our company and as a result were able to compete for almost any marine projects that were either up for tender at that time of those that were being proposed for the next 15 years.

To keep my story tidy I shall provide a description of some of the projects I was actively involved with during my time with GDC after re-joining.

They may, (or may not) include:

- ➢ Doha East Dredging (2007)

- ➢ Dar Salwa (2007)

- ➢ Boubyan Causeway (2010)

- ➢ Salvage of Wrecked Dredger (2010)

- ➢ Boubyan Rock Delivery Jetty (2010)

- ➢ Oman Projects (Barka and Doosan) 2008

- ➢ Sarooj Project in Oman

- ➢ Qatar Projects (Umm Bab Coast Guard Base)

- ➢ Kuwait Armed Forces Officers Club Marina

- ➢ KPA Fish Berths in Shuwaikh Port (2008)

- ➢ Dredging Shuwaikh Channel and Harbour (2)

- ➢ Dredging Shuaiba Port & entrance

- ➢ Saudi Arabia Projects

- ➢ New Split Barge (Design and Build in house)

DOHA EAST DREDGING (2007)

The project came up for tender in 2006 and we purchased the documents. It was a project for the Kuwait Ministry of Electricity and Water. It entailed the dredging of the intake channel at one of the main power stations.

Dredging Scope of Work

> To dredge the Intake Channel for a total length of approximately1650 metres starting one hundred metres from Intake Pump House (ch00) to chainage 1650 metres to Design bed level and slope of 1:4

> The dredged materials shall be deposited for decantation & drying at site and disposed of to the onshore dumping area (within 50 Km from site) approved by Kuwait Municipality.

The intake itself was about 1,750m in length and averaged about 220 metres wide. At the seaward end of the channel there was a barrier with a trash screen that allowed the water to flow in and out with the tide. On top of this barrier there was a roadway connecting each side of the channel.

Pre dredge survey calculations indicated there was around 600,000m3 of sediment to be removed.

This sediment according to our bore hole data was fine grained sandy deposits.

Part of the contract was for the disposal off site of the sedimentary deposits to a place designated by the EPA (Environmental Protection Authority).

My first task was to present a feasibility concept to execute the entire works. Based upon this we then produced our technical bid and our commercial bid of course would then be based upon that.

We eventually decided to use our existing dredger cutter suction *"Arefjan"* rather than go for a dismountable dredger we might hire from another company.

As it happened our decision proved to be the right one for several reasons, not least being the most effective method under the conditions we discovered only when dredging works commenced.

For a start, the materials to be dredged were far more compact than we had determined from the soil analysis and a smaller demountable unit could not have dealt with it effectively.

The first thing I had to do was to figure out how we would get our dredger inside the intake. We had this barrier to deal with before anything else.

After several visits to check the barrier myself, I sat down with my computer and came up with a plan.

At first the Ministry opposed my plan to make an opening in the barrier to allow my equipment inside. But I went to the Under Secretary and eventually convinced him it was either my way or we could not take on the works.

Here below is the general description and basis of my plan for the execution of the project, which after preparation and submittal of extensive details, was finally approved by the Ministry.

1. Prepare the materials for the installation of a temporary trash screen.

2. Install temporary trash screen.

3. Prefabricate the removable panel segments.

4. Prepare the reinforced concrete slabs that form the new road surface.

5. Remove the existing steelwork and piling members.

6. Remove the temporary trash screen.

7. Bring the dredger and marine spread into the intake area.

8. Re-position the temporary trash screen.

9. Dredge the intake area.

10. Handover the intake area to the client.

11. Remove the temporary trash screen.

12. Remove the dredging spread from the intake area.

13. Replace the temporary trash screen.

14. Install the prefabricated units that form the removable insert structure.

15. Install the road surface slabs.

16. Remove the temporary trash screen.

17. Finishing and handing over the entire project site.

I had to sign a guarantee that we would ensure any trash entered the intake between the temporary opening and closing of the intake whilst we moved in our marine equipment and other floating kit would not be allowed to reach the area of the power station.

We finished the works in time and increased our profits by 7% over and above the projected profit. We received from the Ministry a commendation for the works.

Taroob

His Highness the Amir of Kuwait *Sheikh Sabah Al Ahmed Al Hamad Al Sabah* awarded a contract to our company for the restoration of his marina in his summer home in the South of Kuwait.

It entailed dredging the approach channel and the harbour where he has his yachts and other vessels. It was not a very profitable project commercially for us, but it carried a lot of prestige for our company to be selected.

I appointed a very experienced *Project Manager* and personally directed him for the whole of the operation from inception to completion.

Whilst there on my regular daily inspection I was invited to sit at the table of the Emir for lunch.

He was very courteous toward me and even cut me some pieces of fish from a huge Hamour (Grouper), that he had caught himself that very morning.

The project duration was about eleven weeks, and he was happy with the result. He told his Mandoub to give me a model of one of his fishing fleet as a parting gift. The scale model was named after his daughter *Sheikha Salwa*, who sadly died of cancer in her early forties.

The Sheikh never re-married (Nothing like his brother the previous Amir who had married so many times no-one seems to know how many. It is said to be in the hundreds).

Dar Salwa

Most of the time he's in Kuwait, the Emir spends his weekdays in Dar Salwa which is another of his residences. This one is in the district of Salwa.

Poised on the coast it has the usual marina for his boats and for those of his visitors.

GDC were again invited to carry out some works in the marina including installation of hew pontoon modules and some tubular piling and a small amount of maintenance dredging.

Project finished ahead of our projected overall schedule by 42 days. This was due in part to good planning and follow-up on every action throughout the project.

We developed excellent relations with the security personnel at Dar Salwa, which made possible the efficient transit of personnel and equipment into this sensitive area.

Profit margin was anticipated at 19.5% but this was significantly improved due to strategic pricing and efficient overall planning and execution.

We also anticipated that the client would insist upon more than the contract determined.

This was considered during our pricing and because of this we were able to give more than the contract demanded thereby providing a *"hidden discount"* which always leads to client appreciation and benefits the contractor.

Rock Delivery Jetty at Boubyan

As part of our scope of work on this multi-billion-dollar project, GDC were required to prepare a means of receiving over two million tonnes of rock that was to be used in the overall construction of the new port.

A huge fleet of barges would transport the rock. The barges would load in Ras Al Khaima in the United Arab Emirates and travel north by sea to our project site.

My division was charged with the planning and execution of the jetty and the approach to the jetty from the Boubyan Island itself.

We deployed our marine equipment and drove in tubular piles to construct the jetty. Simultaneously, we trucked in tens of thousands of cubic metres of gatch and sand from a designated location in the desert about 110km from the site.

This material was used to construct a temporary causeway to connect the shoreline with the jetty. Owing to the movement of the tides the materials spread significantly.

We knew this would happen of course and allowed for significant losses of materials due to this phenomenon. To minimize the losses, we provided temporary shore protection in the form of quarry run-off stone that was out of specification for permanent works.

Of course, these losses were built into our cost projections and therefore did not impact on our overall plans.

Despite this item of work being under the category of *"Temporary Works,"* compliance with all aspects of the **General Terms and Conditions of Contract** had to be applied.

This meant that all the infill materials had to be according to EPA regulations and of course this all added to our costs. But as with all these types of contracts, the greater the cost of materials the greater the overall profit to the contractor.

This is known as a *"cost-plus-contract"* in industry and because of the nature of the works I was able to obtain this type of agreement for this item.

It was not easy, but the job had to be done, and because it was vital to the WHOLE project, I was given room to maneuver thereby getting a cost-plus agreement. The work was completed on time and within budget.

It should be noted that all the above works were of a temporary nature and would later be demolished when the main project was completed.

Salvage Of Dredger

During the invasion of Kuwait in 1990 by Iraqi armed forces, many pieces of marine equipment were bombed or shelled.

One of these casualties of was a cutter suction dredger owned at the time by a Dutch dredging company. It was engaged at the time on dredging works in the approaches to the Shat-Al-Arab, near to Boubyan Island.

When GDC became involved in the HUGE Boubyan project this wrecked dredger was an impediment to progress and had to be removed. My company asked me to prepare a plan for the removal of the vessel and this I did.

Protocol demanded that before we could even approach the wreck at close quarters the surrounding area had to be checked for unexploded ordnance (EOD). (Explosive Ordnance Demolition

As could be seen, to do this was just hit and miss, and therefore we had to take a risk that our insurance would not cover.

This went to our top management, and they trusted my assessment that we would bring in EOD people throughout the entire process whenever it was a feasible option. There was no other practical way. And so, based upon my plan for removal, we entered negotiations with the client of the project, and after negotiations were awarded the work.

The area where the wreck was positioned was in a tidal zone. The rise and fall averaged around 4.3 metres.

The vessel at some stages of the tide could be approached by waterborne equipment. At these times, the superstructure above water could be cut away and loaded onto a barge.

As the tide receded, the waterborne equipment had to be withdrawn otherwise it could have been damaged by grounding.

This method continued until the operation reached a condition when the next phase of my plane could be started.

We then constructed a temporary band around the wreck using gatch from an approved source. I ensured the bund was of sufficient strength and capacity to allow long boomed excavators and cranes to work from it. It entailed bringing in by truck over 150,000 cubic metres of gatch.

Using high pressure pumps and hoses, the wreck was cleaned incrementally allowing our workforce to cut away piece by piece the remainder of the wreckage.

When this was completed, the bund was removed and I used the gatch materials to supplement the causeway to the rock offloading jetty.

This operation would never win any awards for safety, and it should be said that on several occasions during these operations I had our work permit withdrawn by the main contractor.

But we had to take risks otherwise it could not have been accomplished.

The completion of our work allowed for the construction of the temporary bridge from mainland to Boubyan island to move ahead.

New Split Barges

One item of equipment that we frequently use in dredging operations is a specialized type of barge we call a *split barge*. These *split barges* are primarily used for transportation and dumping at sea of dredged materials.

When our directors appointed a new CEO, he would often consult me on our operational needs and future requirements.

And so, at some point, I was able to convince him that we could use our shipyard facilities to design and construct a couple of large split barges that would enhance our capabilities.

And so, with the expertise of our fabrication personnel, our designers, and the rest, we went ahead and produced two 600m3 capacity split barges.

They were built according to BV standards but unfortunately, we ran severely over budget due to delays caused by design approval from the licensing and insurance people.

Although we used the shipyard facilities of our parent company to construct the vessels, they operated as if we were not related and they did not give us any concessions to the effects of these delays.

It meant that GDC still had to pay for the yard space being used even though the actual assembly work was put on hold whilst the approvals on design were being thrashed out with the licensing authorities like BV, Lloyds, etc.

Our initial commercial benefit projections were revised, and my CEO justifiably blamed me for not warning him of the possibility of these delays.

The truth is that I did not foresee this kind of setback - (related to design) and had I more experience I may have envisaged such possibilities, but I did not.

But as a wiser person once told me, use your mistakes as positive experiences rather than negative ones and it will help in the days to come. So true.

We did in fact build two of these vessels and they were used extensively. We were also able to *"bare boat charter"* these two vessels with **Hyundai** and **Doosan** on projects they had in the **Arabian Gulf.**

We deployed them on many projects whilst I was in the company including Taroob, Shuwaikh Port, Boubyan, Dar Salwa, Fish Berths, etc.

As a result of this venture into design and construction of marine vessels, our parent company - (HEISCO), did in fact embark on other projects in this field and set up a separate division to oversee them.

Small vessels were built including a firefighting vessel for the **Kuwait Fire Services,** a **dive support vessel** for HEISCO, a small aluminium **jet boat** for the Kuwait Ports Authority amongst others.

Shuwaikh Channel Dredging

Project Description

GDC signed a contract on 24th June 2006 with KPA to execute the maintenance dredging of Shuwaikh Channel and Port Basins. This contract was ratified on 28th June 2006, and this was deemed to be the first day of the contract.

The main features of the contract:

Contract Value KD 8,864,159.000 - ($31,524,556.50)

Contract Period. (in two main stages)

1.)Bulk Dredging 12.7 months (382 days)

Value: KD 7,997,431.000 *Maintenance* **Value:** KD 886,415,900

Liquidated Damages Shall be payable at the rate of KD 500.000 per day ($1,750.00)

Dredging Quantity (m3) BOQ 1,223,418 Take Off 1,138,713 Spoil Disposal Area 19 nautical miles distance from port.

During the tendering process, I requested our HR dept. to find us a good project manager for this project.

After interviewing several people, I selected a man who had an impressive record with Osman Al Osman, a very large dredging company who was involved in many projects in the Middle East including the Suez Canal widening.

This man was an Egyptian gentleman who initially impressed me, but who turned out to be something other than what I had expected. His name was **Hesham......** *?????,* a name I shall never forget.

The project began quite well as we had prepared everything professionally and it followed our project plan nicely.

But after about a month, I could see that I was spending more time myself in a ***"hands on"*** situation on this project. As Division Manager, I had several projects running at the same time of course, and when I was spending as much time as I was on this project, it left less time for me to focus on other matters.

And so, I brought in another engineer to supplement the work but of course, this was outside of the project budget and so we had to ensure this did not impact our overall strategy on profit.

Hesham was reluctant to work 7 days a week as he'd initially agreed to do. Being a salaried member of our company, he like the rest of us would not be paid overtime. Our efforts were assessed annually, and our bonuses were evaluated upon our results.

Under the labour laws, I was powerless to enforce anyone to work longer hours than the law allowed. But in Kuwait in those times, we all worked many hours. In fact, even as Division Manager, I would spend an AVERAGE of 80 hours weekly at my work.

When I had efficient project managers handling the day-to-day affairs on any project it was a world away from a project manager not pulling his weight. And this was how **Hesham** was performing - 60% of what was required.

A unique feature of this project was a clause whereby my company had to impart training to 12 of the client personnel in the art of dredging. This was left entirely to me as to how to impart such training.

I would arrange for these client personnel to spend time on the vessels and time in the classroom with me.

I would also use the Conference Room in our office building to give presentations to these trainees. I wanted to show them enough to keep them reasonably satisfied *but not too much to give away all our techniques and competitive strategies.*

And so, it was a bit of a juggling act, but we got through it. Whether or not those trainees ever gained from the experience I nether know nor care. To me it was just another part of the job.

This project overran on time, and I had many meetings with the KPA management. The Chairman of KPA at the time was a brother of the ruler- (H.H.Sheikh Sabah Al Ahmad).

This man was a very powerful and very difficult person to deal with. I had met him on several occasions at meetings. His name was *Sheikh Sabah Jaber Al-Ali Al Sabah,* and he was the *Director General of Kuwait Ports Authority*.

Powerful and influential and with the arrogance that often goes with people in such posts, he was THE MAN when it came to do with anything in Kuwait Ports.

During this project, my Chairman Mr. Manaf Al Hanna, was summoned to a meeting with the Sheikh. It was connected to the project in the port that was behind schedule at that point. The Chairman called our General Manager at the time - (Mr Rafiq), along with me and the project Manager (Hesham) to his office.

We briefed him on the project details, and he instructed me as Head of Marine Operations to be the speaker at the meeting. I was astonished at this because he was our *chairman* and senior to us all. And it was himself to whom the letter from the Sheikh was addressed.

I was never nervous of meeting these members of the Royal family and my chairman was aware of this. But I respectfully pointed out the Manaf, that if he did not lead our small delegation, it would appear as a weakness on our part.

He pushed this reasoning aside in the argument that I had more experience than anyone in the company on dredging operations, and this project was primarily a dredging operation.

And with this decision being made, we attended the meeting.

We attended on time at the conference room at the Port Administration Building. As is not uncommon with arrogant people, he kept us waiting in the reception room for almost 2 hours.

When we were eventually invited around the conference table, the Sheikh, without even apologising for keeping us waiting, started his attack.

He was surrounded by his cronies including the harbour master, his lawyer, private secretary, engineers, harbour pilots and others.

He started by slagging off our company in general saying we were taking money from the Authority and giving poor performance.

This was only partly true, (the poor performance part - at this stage of the works), but taking money – definitely not. He was not signing the cheques and so our money was being held.

After a while he started slagging off our General Manager with *a savage personal attack*. I felt so embarrassed for him and angry at this bully. My GM just sat there *like a sheep* and did not even try to retaliate. Our chairman too said nothing, just looking embarrassed.

At this point I had heard all I was going to let my ears take in. I wanted to tell the Sheikh exactly what I thought of him but *somehow controlled my inner rage*.

Instead, I started to gather my papers before me and put them into my briefcase. The Sheikh looked over to me and scowled. I looked right back at him with contempt.

I then stood up and said, *"Gentlemen, that's all I am prepared to take away from this meeting. Good day"*

I was hoping my chairman would also leave with me and then the other two would follow. but he just sat there with the others in our delegation.

I waited for a minute or two outside of the Conference Room but all I could hear was the rantings of the Sheikh.

Knowing the Sheikhs predisposition to rages, I was expecting the worst and in truth was more than a little apprehensive. These people have so much power that upsetting one of them could lead to finding yourself in the remote desert up to your neck in sand. *I kid you not.*

But I walked back to my car. The main gate was closed as it was after 14:30 and so I had to drive all through the port to find a gate that was used by the cargo trucks.

I went back to my office, not knowing what the repercussions would be. I left for home soon afterwards.

The following morning as soon as the Chairman came to his office, I went to talk to him.

He was undoubtedly embarrassed by what had happened at the meeting but told me he had great respect for my courage and actions.

He explained that he had to stay behind and listen to more of the Sheik's rantings, but he let the storm blow itself out and at the end of the meeting he had a private meeting with the Sheikh.

Although Manaf did not confide in me any of the details, I concluded that at this private meeting, he had satisfied the Sheikh in some way so that the project could proceed. You may draw your own conclusions.

That may seem in the western world as corrupt and totally illegal, but it is in fact the way things work in the Middle East. And in truth, it's not confined to those countries but can be found all over, including UK.

The project overran the schedule by 46 days, and a penalty of KD 23,000.000 (equivalent to $76,750.00) was imposed on us.

We mounted a legal challenge to this, and the damages were eventually reduced to ten percent of the sum. But this took almost 3 years before the KPA returned the monies they had held back.

As a maritime company, we were very fortunate to have a superb base in the Port of Shuwaikh where our parent company HEISCO had a shipyard, a drydock and a synchro-lift.

This truly added a very sharp edge to our competitiveness in the country when it came to logistics.

But there was a drawback. This was because the KPA (Kuwait Ports Authority) had us over a barrel because our yards lay in the jurisdiction area that was under KPA care and control.

And the Sheikh knew very well of our reliance on the Authority, and he used it to coerce us in any way he thought would be to his advantage.

CHAPTER 10 - Health Issues

I was involved in more than a dozen projects in the ports of Kuwait during my time there and not even one of them was easy.

I must mention that GDC gave me every opportunity to develop a varied and interesting career. For that I am truly grateful.

I began as a second dredge master and finished at my retirement as Manager of the Offshore Works & Dredging Division. I enjoyed almost everything I was involved with and learned so much from the experience.

In 2011, as the result of a heart attack that almost ended my life, I decided that it was time to let go of full-time employment and see what retirement had to offer. After having surgery and a short convalescence period, I returned to my desk and submitted my resignation.

As a result, my chairman at the time, Mr. Manaf Al-Muhanna came to my office and was reluctant to accept my resignation. He kindly offered for me to stay on as a consultant if I preferred.

I declined the generous offer as I told him it was time for me to go into retirement. I felt that I was now in my seventy-fist year, and my health was not guaranteed.

I stayed a little longer than I had planned because the company had been so good to me but after serving out my minimum notice of 3 months, I eventually left the company in 2012. June and I stayed on in Kuwait until October 2017 before returning to our little council house in Scotland.

Retirement And All That Stuff

We had to sell and give away almost everything we had gathered over our years in Kuwait because we had nowhere in Scotland that could accommodate the stuff.

We brought back to Scotland just a few of the smaller things that could be packed into 4 suitcases and the rest we left behind. It is always hard to do this, and we have over the last 40 years had to do similar exercises on several occasions.

At first, June was not too happy as she wanted a more spacious place for us to live with perhaps another bedroom.

I argued as to why we needed another bedroom as we have only had two visitors in the 16 years we have lived here. And buying a place was not the best way forward as it would mean liquidating our pension fund.

Because I had been an expatriate worker and living abroad for the best part of the past 41 years, I had not fully contributed to the UK state pension scheme. As such my entitlement to any state benefit was severely compromised. So, we had to carefully budget our living costs.

June was drawing a state pension of about £ 319.00 per month.

We had savings which we had to rely upon for day to day living but we had to be careful of course. But we decided to spend some of our savings to improve our lives in our home. And so, we began to make improvements to our one-bedroom council house.

This included splashing out for a summer house in the garden. This enabled us to move stuff out of our bedroom to create more space. We bought a new cooker and put new tiles on the kitchen floor. We bought a new mattress for our bed. **Scott** bought us a new chair for the living room, and we also purchased a similar one.

We made a few small improvements elsewhere and within 12 months our little place was transformed. We bought some floor to ceiling sliding doors and got someone in to fit them in the bedroom which made a huge difference. The wardrobes that had been in that space I put into our summer house. We used them for added storage facility.

We put in a new fence between ours and the next-door neighbour and the decking made so much difference on nice days where we can sit out with a cuppa and a biscuit.

June still does **voluntary** unpaid work for the **British Heart Foundation.** She normally spends time helping at the shop in the city.

We don't have a car nowadays as it's a bit outside of our means. We mange very well with the **local bus service** and we are fortunate enough to have a **bus pass** which allows us to travel by bus anywhere in Scotland for free - (well almost).

We often travel off to Glasgow or sometimes Aberdeen in addition to Dingwall on the Black Isle or Nairn Forres and Elgin too. We are very grateful to have had such full and enjoyable lives.

Like almost everyone, we have had our tough times and our easy times. Overall, I feel very blessed to have had such an interesting life presented to me. I could have missed it. Looking back to my early years, I seemed to have a selfish approach to life in general. I had little or no ambition except perhaps to have as much fun as I could.

I think that is not unusual for many young people, but I have learned in later years that self-centred behaviour can be the root cause of inner turmoil and unless dealt with can lead to unhappiness and restlessness. At least, that is my own experience.

There were so many times in my life that I made mistakes that would cause pain and anguish to myself and to others. These others did not deserve this, and this guilt led my inner self to feel ashamed and regretful.

But pain is said to be the touchstone of all spiritual growth and something that can paradoxically turn out to be a real friend.

As for the fellowship of Alcoholics Anonymous, it almost certainly saved my life and in fact opened a dimension of living that I had never thought possible.

On most days I have a peace within that defies all understanding, but I put this down to living in a way that AA has taught me. In 2011, I had a quite serious heart attack and thanks to the skills of doctors, surgeons and hospital staff, I got through it virtually unscathed. But it was also a wake-up-call to remind me that life is unpredictable, precious and that tomorrow is not guaranteed.

And so, it got my thoughts directed to my grandchildren who in all honesty hardly know me or anything about my family, except what they may have heard from elsewhere.

I never knew a grandmother, grandfather, aunt, uncle, cousin or any blood relations except for my own mum and dad and siblings.

I then thought it would be unfair for my own grandchildren not to know about their own grandad and so the best way to remedy this is to put pen to paper. This is the result.

And so, with that, I am going to finish this document and prepare it to pass on to my grandchildren.

I dedicate this overview of my family and my life up to today to the *"love of my life"*.............. JUNE.

She has been, and remains, my rock and my life has been richer because of her.

Thank you darling............. for everything.   September 2019.

Contents

ABOUT THE AUTHOR. For more than four decades and multiple continents. He has worked on major maritime and infrastructure projects across the United Kingdom, Europe, the Middle East, and North America, often in politically sensitive and high-risk environments. During the 1990 Iraqi invasion of Kuwait, he was taken hostage and later returned to the region to assist with post-war reconstruction. His work placed him in close proximity to both historical events and the people affected by them.

Printed in Dunstable, United Kingdom

76244808R00097